CONTENTS

Chapter One: An Overview

Terrorism	1
Types of terrorism	2
Fear of terrorism	3
A brief history of terrorism	5
Methods of attack	9
Terrorism: the problems of definition	10
The war against terrorism	13
The unrealistic war on terror	14
Terrorists and suicide attacks	15
Think again: Al Qaeda	17
The European Union response to terrorism	19
Terrorism and the EU	19
Targeting terrorist funds	22
At the service of politicians	23
Threat of terrorism	23
Ability to reason vital in fighting terrorism	24
What does Islam say about terrorism?	26

Chapter Two: Terrorism and the UK

Who are the terrorists?	27
'We must unite to defeat this threat'	28
Home Office draw up tighter terrorism laws	30
Terrorism	31
Counter-terrorism and resilience: key facts	33
MI5 website lists 10 anti-terrorist tips	34
Internment in Britain	35
Countering terrorism	35
Islamophobia – what is it?	36
Islam: a home of tolerance, not fanaticism	37
Terrorism – what you can do at home	38
Travelling	39
Key Facts	40
Additional Resources	41
Index	42
Acknowledgements	44

Introduction

Terrorism is the ninety-second volume in the **Issues** series. The aim of this series is to offer up-to-date information about important issues in our world.

Terrorism looks at the threat of terrorism globally and in the UK.

The information comes from a wide variety of sources and includes:
Government reports and statistics
Newspaper reports and features
Magazine articles and surveys
Website material
Literature from lobby groups
and charitable organisations.

It is hoped that, as you read about the many aspects of the issues explored in this book, you will critically evaluate the information presented. It is important that you decide whether you are being presented with facts or opinions. Does the writer give a biased or an unbiased report? If an opinion is being expressed, do you agree with the writer?

Terrorism offers a useful starting-point for those who need convenient access to information about the many issues involved. However, it is only a starting-point. At the back of the book is a list of organisations which you may want to contact for further information.

*****

Terrorism

ISSUES

Volume 92

Editor

Craig Donnellan

Independence

Educational Publishers
Cambridge

First published by Independence
PO Box 295
Cambridge CB1 3XP
England

British Library Cataloguing in Publication Data
Terrorism – (Issues Series)
I. Donnellan, Craig II. Series
303.6'25

ISBN 1 86168 300 6

Printed in Great Britain
MWL Print Group Ltd

Typeset by
Claire Boyd

Cover
The illustration on the front cover is by
Simon Kneebone.

Terrorism

An introduction

Is terrorism just brutal, unthinking violence?

No. Experts agree that there is almost always a strategy behind terrorist actions. Whether it takes the form of bombings, shootings, hijackings, or assassinations, terrorism is neither random, spontaneous, nor blind; it is a deliberate use of violence against civilians for political or religious ends.

Is there a definition of terrorism?

Even though most people can recognise terrorism when they see it, experts have had difficulty coming up with an ironclad definition. The US State Department defines terrorism as 'premeditated, politically motivated violence perpetrated against noncombatant targets by subnational groups or clandestine agents, usually intended to influence an audience'. In another useful attempt to produce a definition, Paul Pillar, a former deputy chief of the CIA's Counterterrorist Center, argues that there are four key elements of terrorism:

1. It is premeditated – planned in advance, rather than an impulsive act of rage.
2. It is political – not criminal, like the violence that groups such as the mafia use to get money, but designed to change the existing political order.
3. It is aimed at civilians – not at military targets or combat-ready troops.
4. It is carried out by subnational groups – not by the army of a country.

Where does the word 'terrorism' come from?

It was coined during France's Reign of Terror in 1793-94. Originally, the leaders of this systematised attempt to weed out 'traitors' among the revolutionary ranks praised terror as the best way to defend liberty, but as the French Revolution soured, the word soon took on grim echoes of state violence and guillotines. Today, most terrorists dislike the label, according to Bruce Hoffman of the RAND Corporation think tank (www.rand.org).

Is terrorism a new phenomenon?

No. The oldest terrorists were holy warriors who killed civilians. For instance, in first-century Palestine, Jewish Zealots would publicly slit the throats of Romans and their collaborators; in seventh-century India, the Thuggee cult would ritually strangle passers-by as sacrifices to the Hindu deity Kali; and in the eleventh-century Middle East, the Shiite sect known as the Assassins would eat hashish before murdering

> *Terrorist acts are often deliberately spectacular, designed to rattle and influence a wide audience, beyond the victims of the violence itself*

civilian foes. Historians can trace recognisably modern forms of terrorism back to such late-nineteenth-century organisations as Narodnaya Volya ('People's Will'), an anti-tsarist group in Russia. One particularly successful early case of terrorism was the 1914 assassination of Austrian Archduke Franz Ferdinand by a Serb extremist, an event that helped trigger World War I. Even more familiar forms of terrorism – often custom-made for TV cameras – first appeared on 22 July 1968, when the Popular Front for the Liberation of Palestine undertook the first terrorist hijacking of a commercial airplane.

Is terrorism aimed at an audience?

Usually, yes. Terrorist acts are often deliberately spectacular, designed to rattle and influence a wide audience, beyond the victims of the violence itself. The point is to use the psychological impact of violence or of the threat of violence to effect political change. As the terrorism expert Brian Jenkins bluntly put it in 1974, 'Terrorism is theatre.'

TERRORISTS CAN TURN ALMOST ANYTHING INTO A WEAPON...

Types of terrorism

Information from the Council on Foreign Relations

Are there different types of terrorism?

Yes. While these categories are not written in stone, experts have identified at least six different sorts of terrorism: nationalist, religious, state-sponsored, left-wing, right-wing, and anarchist.

What is nationalist terrorism?

Nationalist terrorists seek to form a separate state for their own national group, often by drawing attention to a fight for 'national liberation' that they think the world has ignored. This sort of terrorism has been among the most successful at winning international sympathy and concessions. Experts say that nationalist terror groups have tended to calibrate their use of violence, using enough to rivet world attention but not so much that they alienate supporters abroad or members of their base community. Nationalist terrorism can be difficult to define, since many groups accused of the practice insist that they are not terrorists but freedom fighters.

What are some examples of nationalist terrorist groups?

Nationalist terrorist groups include the Irish Republican Army and the Palestine Liberation Organisation, both of which said during the 1990s that they had renounced terrorism. Other prominent examples are the Basque Fatherland and Liberty, which seeks to create a Basque homeland separate from Spain, and the Kurdistan Workers' Party, which seeks to create a Kurdish state independent from Turkey. Earlier nationalist terror groups sought to expel colonial rulers; such groups included the Irgun and the Lehi (both Jewish militias opposed to British rule in Palestine in the 1940s) and the National Liberation Front (opposed to French rule in Algeria in the 1950s).

What is religious terrorism?

Religious terrorists seek to use violence to further what they see as divinely commanded purposes, often targeting broad categories of foes in an attempt to bring about sweeping changes. Religious terrorists come from many major faiths, as well as from small cults. This type of terrorism is growing swiftly, notes Bruce Hoffman of the RAND think tank; in 1995 (the most recent year for which such statistics were available), nearly half of the 56 known, active international terrorist groups were religiously motivated. Because religious terrorists are concerned not with rallying a constituency of fellow nationalists or ideologues but with pursuing their own vision of the divine will, they lack one of the major constraints that historically has limited the scope of terror attacks, experts say. As Hoffman puts it, the most extreme religious terrorists can sanction 'almost limitless violence against a virtually open-ended category of targets: that is, anyone who is not a member of the terrorists' religion or religious sect'.

What are some examples of religious terrorist groups?

Examples include Osama bin Laden's al-Qaeda network, the Palestinian Sunni Muslim organization Hamas, the Lebanese Shiite group Hezbollah, the radical Jewish groups affiliated with the late Rabbi Meir Kahane, the Israeli extremists Baruch Goldstein (who machine-gunned

> *Experts have identified at least six different sorts of terrorism: nationalist, religious, state-sponsored, left-wing, right-wing, and anarchist*

Muslim worshippers in a Hebron mosque in 1994) and Yigal Amir (who assassinated then Prime Minister Yitzhak Rabin in 1995), some American white-supremacist militias, and the Aum Shinrikyo doomsday cult in Japan.

What is state-sponsored terrorism?
State-sponsored terrorist groups are deliberately used by radical states as foreign policy tools – as Hoffman puts it, as 'a cost-effective way of waging war covertly, through the use of surrogate warriors or "guns for hire"'. One important early case was the Iranian government's use of supposedly independent young militants to seize hostages at the American embassy in Tehran in 1979. With enhanced resources at their disposal, state-sponsored terrorist groups are often capable of carrying out more deadly attacks than other terrorists, including airplane bombings.

Fear of terrorism

Similar levels of fear of terrorism in USA and Great Britain. But Americans are more confident than the British in their government's ability to reduce likelihood of terrorist attack

By Humphrey Taylor

A new poll by Harris Interactive® in the United States and its subsidiary HI Europe in the United Kingdom finds that the levels of anxiety about possible terrorist attacks in the two allied nations are very similar, as are the generally modest proportions of people who have changed their behaviour because of the fear of terrorism. There is, however, one clear difference. Americans have more confidence than the British in the ability of the government to reduce the likelihood of a terrorist attack.

How much do people worry about a possible terrorist attack?
Most people in both countries do not worry a lot about a possible attack. People in Great Britain are slightly more worried than Americans about the possibility of a terrorist attack somewhere in the country, but the difference is very small. Twelve per cent (12%) of the British, compared to 9% of Americans, worry 'often', while 59% of the British worry 'occasionally' or 'often' compared to 55% in the United States.

However, the more important finding here is that large numbers in both countries don't worry much or at all (45% in the US and 41% in GB) and that only small minorities in both countries worry 'often'.

The likelihood of a major terrorist attack?
Public expectations about the likelihood of a major terrorist attack are closely related, unsurprisingly, to their level of anxiety. In both the United States and in Great Britain, only 11% think a major attack is 'very' likely in the next twelve months, but most people (62% in the US and 64% in GB) think it is either 'somewhat' or 'very' likely.

What people are doing to reduce their own risk
Large majorities in both countries say they are not making any changes in their travel plans, their visits to big cities, or to big sporting or other events because of the possibilities of a terrorist attack.

However, even small percentages represent millions of people, so fear of terrorism is having some impact on behaviour:

- 11% in the US and 10% in GB say they are avoiding travelling by air 'a lot.'
- 7% in both countries say they are avoiding big sporting or other events 'a lot.'
- 5% in the US and 3% in GB say they are travelling 'a lot' less.
- 5% in US and 6% in GB say they are avoiding visiting big cities 'a lot'.

Confidence in the government's ability to reduce likelihood of terrorist attack?
British and American perceptions of risk and their modest 'avoidance behaviour' are extraordinarily similar. However, their confidence in their governments to protect them from terrorist attacks are different. In the United States, 72% of adults have at least some confidence in the ability of the government to reduce the likelihood of terrorist attacks. In Britain, only a more modest 54% have at least some confidence. In Britain, 46% have little or no confidence in their government's ability to reduce the risk, compared to only 28% in the United States.

These results are based on parallel surveys of the public conducted online. The US survey is based on 3,378 adults aged 18 and over interviewed between January 19 and 28, 2004. The Great Britain survey is based on 2,417 people aged 18 and over surveyed between January 21 and 26, 2004.

Worries about possibility of terrorist attacks

'How often do you worry about the possibility of a terrorist attack in this country?'

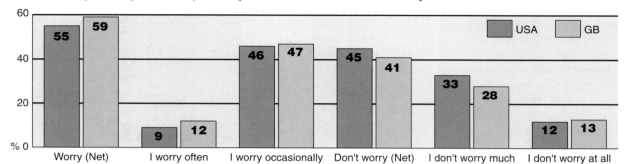

Base: All adults
Note: Percentages may not add up exactly to rounding

Likelihood of terrorist attack in this country in the next twelve months

'How likely do you think it is that there will be a major terrorist attack in this country in the next twelve months?'

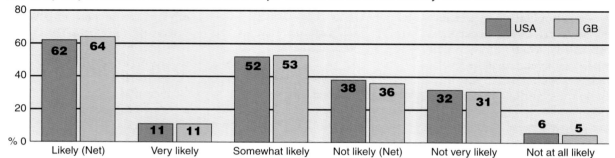

Base: All adults
Note: Percentages may not add up exactly to rounding

Things which will be avoided because of possible terrorist attack

'To what extent do you think you do the following because of the possibility of a terrorist attack?'

	A lot	Some	Not at all	Not sure
Avoid travelling by air				
USA	11%	16%	68%	5%
GB	10%	17%	68%	5%
Avoid big sporting or other events				
USA	7%	11%	78%	4%
GB	7%	14%	73%	5%
Travel less				
USA	5%	14%	77%	3%
GB	3%	14%	78%	4%
Avoid visiting big cities				
USA	5%	12%	79%	4%
GB	6%	18%	72%	3%

Base: All adults
Note: Percentages may not add up exactly to rounding

Confidence in government's ability to reduce likelihood of terrorist attack

'How much confidence do you have in the ability of the government to reduce the likelihood of a terrorist attack?'

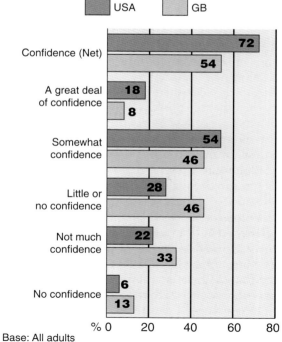

Base: All adults
Note: Percentages may not add up exactly to rounding

Methodology for Harris Interactive US poll

The Harris Poll® was conducted online within the United States between January 19 and 28, 2004 among a nationwide cross section of 3,378 adults. Figures for age, sex, race, education, income and region were weighted where necessary to bring them into line with their actual proportions in the population. 'Propensity score' weighting was also used to adjust for respondents' propensity to be online.

In theory, with probability samples of this size, one could say with 95 per cent certainty that the results have a statistical precision of plus or minus 1.7 percentage points of what they would be if the entire adult population had been polled with complete accuracy. Unfortunately, there are several other possible sources of error in all polls or surveys that are probably more serious than theoretical calculations of sampling error. They include refusals to be interviewed (non-response), question wording and question order, and weighting. It is impossible to quantify the errors that may result from these factors. This online sample is not a probability sample.

These statements conform to the principles of disclosure of the National Council on Public Polls.

Methodology for HI Europe Great Britain Poll

This HI Europe survey was conducted online within Great Britain between January 21 and January 26, 2004 among 2,417 Britons, aged 18 and older. Figures for age, sex, education, income and region were weighted where necessary to bring them into line with their actual proportions in the population. 'Propensity score' weighting was also used to adjust for respondents' propensity to be online.

In theory, with probability samples of this size, one could say with 95 per cent certainty that the results have a statistical precision of plus or minus 2 percentage points of what they would be if the entire adult population had been polled with complete accuracy. Unfortunately,

there are several other possible sources of error in all polls or surveys that are probably more serious than theoretical calculations of sampling error. They include refusals to be interviewed (non-response), question wording and question order, and weighting. It is impossible to quantify the errors that may result from these factors. This online sample is not a probability sample.

Humphrey Taylor is the chairman of The Harris Poll®, Harris Interactive.

■ The above information is from Harris Interactive's website: www.harrisinteractive.com

A brief history of terrorism

Information from the Center for Defense Information

By Mark Burgess

To begin any history of terrorism (however brief) without first defining what the term means might appear to be putting the cart before the horse. Despite this, no such definition shall be proffered here.[1] Partly, this is for reasons of brevity, but mainly because any effort to first define terrorism would mean restricting any ensuing narrative to this definition. As such, this is not so much a brief history of terrorism as much as a brief history of examples of that which has been (or arguably could be) generally accepted to

constitute terrorism. Not everyone will agree that all these examples do so, and there are other instances that could be so construed that are not mentioned at all.

One point is less debatable: terrorism is not new. Indeed, in some respects, what is today known as terrorism predates by millennia the modern term used to describe it. This

is not to say that the act of terrorism has remained static. Rather, as the difficulties involved in defining it reflect, terrorism has evolved considerably over the years, even if retaining some of the same characteristics that have historically typified it.

While it is impossible to definitively ascertain when it was first used, that which we today call terrorism traces its roots back at least some 2,000 years. Moreover, today's terrorism has, in some respects, come full circle, with many of its contemporary practitioners motivated by religious convictions – something which drove many of their earliest predecessors. It has also, in the generally accepted usage of the word, often possessed a political dimension. This has coloured much of the discourse surrounding terrorism – a phenomenon which is, according to Paul R. Pillar, 'a challenge to be managed, not solved'.[2]

Religious roots[3]

Among the earliest such examples were the Sicari and the Zealots, Jewish groups active during the Roman occupation of the first-century Middle East. The favoured weapon of the Sicari was the *sica* (the short dagger which gave them their name, which literally means 'dagger men'), which they used to murder those (mainly Jews) they deemed apostate and thus selected for execution. The Zealots, who generally targeted Romans and Greeks, give us the modern term Zealot, one translation of which is 'a fanatical partisan'.[4] Such killings usually took place in daylight and in front of witnesses, with the perpetrators using such acts to send a message to the Roman authorities and those Jews who collaborated with them – a tactic that would also be used by subsequent generations of what would become known as terrorists.

Adherents of other religions also resorted to methods which might today be termed terrorism, such as the Assassins – an 11th-century offshoot of a Shia Muslim sect known as the Ismailis. Like the Zealots-Sicari, the Assassins were also given to stabbing their victims (generally politicians or clerics who refused to adopt the purified version of Islam they were forcibly spreading) in broad daylight.[5] The Assassins – whose name gave us the modern term but literally meant 'hashish-eater' – a reference to the ritualistic drug-taking they were (perhaps falsely) rumoured to indulge in prior to undertaking missions – also used their actions to send a message.[6] Often, the Assassins' deeds were carried out at religious sites on holy days – a tactic intended to publicise their cause and incite others to it. Like many religiously inspired terrorists today, they also viewed their deaths on such operations as sacrificial and a guarantor that they would enter paradise.

One point is less debatable: terrorism is not new. Indeed, in some respects, what is today known as terrorism predates by millennia the modern term used to describe it

---

Sacrifice was also a central element of the killings carried out by the Thuggees (who bequeathed us the word 'thug') – an Indian religious cult who ritually strangled their victims (usually travellers chosen at random) as an offering to the Hindu goddess of terror and destruction, Kali. In this case, the intent was to terrify the victim (a vital consideration in the Thuggee ritual) rather than influence any external audience.

Active from the seventh until the mid-19th centuries, the Thuggees are reputed to be responsible for as many as 1 million murders. They were perhaps the last example of religiously-inspired terrorism until the phenomenon reemerged a little over 20 years ago. As David Rapoport puts it: 'Before the 19th century, religion provided the only acceptable justifications for terror.'[7] More secularised motivations for such actions did not emerge until the French Revolution, as did the first usage of the term now used to describe them.

Nationalists and anarchists

The English word 'terrorism' comes from the *régime de la terreur* that prevailed in France from 1793-1794. Originally an instrument of the state, the regime was designed to consolidate the power of the newly-installed revolutionary government, protecting it from elements considered 'subversive'. Always value-laden, terrorism was, initially, a positive term. The French revolutionary leader, Maximilien Robespierre, viewed it as vital if the new French Republic was to survive its infancy, proclaiming in 1794 that:

'Terror is nothing other than justice, prompt, severe, inflexible; it is therefore an emanation of virtue; it is not so much a special principle as it is a consequence of the general principle of democracy applied to our country's most urgent needs.'[8]

Under such justification, some 40,000 people were executed by guillotine – a fate Robespierre and his top lieutenants would themselves suffer when later that same year, his announcement of a new list of subversives led to a counter-inquisition by some in the Revolutionary government who feared their names might be on the latest roll of 'traitors'. Before long, the Revolution devoured itself in an orgy of paranoiac bloodletting. Meanwhile, terrorism itself began taking on the negative connotations it carries today (terrorists do not generally tend to describe themselves thus), helped initially by the writings of those like the British political philosopher Edmund Burke, who popularised the term 'terrorism' in English while demonising its French revolutionary practitioners.

The newly defined notions of nationalism and citizenship, which both caused and were a result of the French Revolution, also saw the emergence of a new predominantly secular terrorism. The appearance of political ideologies such as Marxism also created a fertile sense of unrest at the existing order, with terrorism offering a means for change. The Italian revolutionary Carlo Pisacane's theory of the 'propaganda of the deed' – which recognised the utility of terrorism to deliver a message to an audience other than the target and draw attention and support to a cause – typified this new form of terrorism.[9]

Pisacane's thesis – which was not in itself new and would probably have been recognisable to the Zealots-Sicari and the Assassins – was first put into practice by the Narodnaya Volya (NV), a Russian Populist group (whose name translates as the People's Will) formed in 1878 to oppose the Tsarist regime. The group's most famous deed, the assassination of Alexander II on 1 March, 1881, also effectively sealed their fate by incurring the full

wrath of the Tsarist regime. Unlike most other terrorist groups, the NV went to great lengths to avoid 'innocent' deaths, carefully choosing their targets – usually state officials who symbolised the regime – and often compromising operations rather than causing what would today be termed 'collateral damage'.

The NV's actions inspired radicals elsewhere. Anarchist terrorist groups were particularly enamoured of the example set by the Russian Populists (although not, it must be noted, their keenness to avoid casualties among bystanders). Nationalist groups such as those in Ireland and the Balkans adopted terrorism as a means towards their desired ends. As the 19th century gave way to the 20th, terrorist attacks were carried out as far afield as India, Japan, and the Ottoman empire, with two US presidents and a succession of other world leaders victims of assassination by various anarchists and other malcontents – often affiliated to groups but operating without their explicit knowledge or support.[10]

As with Europe, terrorism arrived on America's shores before the 20th century. Not only were Anarchists active in America throughout the 1880s, but the country's recent Civil War had seen acts deserving of the name committed on both sides as well as the formation of the Ku Klux Klan to fight the Reconstruction effort which followed.[11]

Terrorism and the State

Long before the outbreak of Word War I in Europe in 1914, what would later be termed state-sponsored terrorism had already started to manifest itself. For instance, many officials in the Serbian government and military were involved (albeit unofficially) in supporting, training and arming the various Balkan groups which were active prior to the assassination of the Archduke Franz Ferdinand on 28 June 1914 in Sarajevo – an act carried out by an activist from one such group, the 'Young Bosnians' and credited with setting in progress the chain of events which led to the war itself.[12] Similarly, the IMRO (Macedonian Revolutionary Organisation) survived largely 'because [as Walter Laqueur reminds us] it became for all intents and purposes a tool of the Bulgarian government, and was used mainly against Yugoslavia as well as against domestic enemies'. As such examples illustrate, state-sponsored terrorism is not a new phenomenon.

The 1930s saw a fresh wave of political assassinations deserving of the word terrorism. This led to proposals at the League of Nations for conventions to prevent and punish terrorism as well as the establishment of an international criminal court (neither of which came to aught as they were overshadowed by the events which eventually led to World War II).[13] Despite this, during the interwar years, terrorism increasingly referred to the oppressive measures imposed by various totalitarian regimes, most notably those in Nazi Germany, Fascist Italy and Stalinist Russia. More recently, other governments, such as those military dictatorships which ruled some South American countries in recent years, or the current regime in Zimbabwe, have also been open to charges of using such methods as a tool of state. Such considerations notwithstanding, some commentators, such as Bruce Hoffman, argue that 'such usages are generally termed "terror" in order to distinguish that phenomenon from "terrorism," which is understood to be violence committed by non-state entities'.[14] However, not everyone agrees that terrorism should be considered a non-governmental undertaking.

For instance, Jessica Stern insists that in deliberately bombarding civilians as a means of attacking enemy morale, states have indeed resorted to terrorism. Per Stern, such instances include not only the Allied strategic bombing campaigns of World War II, but the American dropping of atomic bombs on Hiroshima and Nagasaki that ended the Pacific phase of that conflict.[15] This issue remains a contentious one, with individuals such as the World War II British Air Chief, 'Bomber' Harris, alternatively defended and reviled for their belief in the utility and morality of strategic bombing.

Contemporary terrorism

Today, terrorism influences events on the international stage to a degree hitherto unachieved. Largely, this is due to the attacks of September 2001. Since then, in the United States at least, terrorism has largely been equated to the threat posed by al Qaeda – a threat inflamed not only by the spectacular and deadly nature of the Sept. 11 attacks themselves, but by the fear that future strikes might be even more deadly and employ weapons of mass destruction.

Whatever global threat may be posed by al Qaeda and its franchisees, the US view of terrorism nonetheless remains, to a degree, largely ego-centric – despite the current administration's rhetoric concerning a so-called 'Global War Against Terrorism'. This is far from unique. Despite the implications that al Qaeda actually intends to wage a global insurgency, the citizens of countries such as Colombia or Northern Ireland (to name but two of those long faced with terrorism) are likely more preoccupied with when and where the next FARC or Real Irish Republican Army attack will occur rather than where the next al Qaeda strike will fall.

As such considerations indicate, terrorism goes beyond al Qaeda, which it not only predates but will also outlive. Given this, if terrorism is to be countered most effectively, any understanding of it must go beyond the threat currently posed by that particular organisation. Without such a broad-based approach, not only will terrorism be unsolvable (to paraphrase Pillar) but it also risks becoming unmanageable.

References

1 The question of how to define terrorism warrants deeper discussion than is possible here. As such, a subsequent paper in CDI's *Explaining Terrorism* series shall address this topic.
2 Paul R. Pillar, *Terrorism and US Foreign Policy*, Brookings Institute Press: Washington, DC, 2001, p. vii.
3 For a fuller discussion of the three groups discussed in this section see David C. Rapoport, 'Fear and Trembling: Terrorism in Three Religious Traditions,' *American Political Science Review*, Vol. 78, No. 3 (September 1984), pp. 668-672.
4 *Webster's Third New International Dictionary* (Merriam-Webster, 1984), p. 2657.
5 That no contemporaneous Christian terrorist groups are considered here reflects the fact that no such group easily lends itself to a comparative analysis. As Rapoport puts it: 'Their

---

Today, terrorism influences events on the international stage to a degree hitherto unachieved. Largely, this is due to the attacks of September 2001

[millenarian Christian groups of the late Medieval period] terror was a sort of state terror; the sects organized their communities openly, taking full control of a territory, instituting gruesome purges to obliterate all traces of the old order, and organizing large armies, which waged holy wars periodically sweeping over the countryside and devastating, burning, and massacring everything and everyone in their paths,' Rapoport, op cit. p. 660, n. 4.
6 According to Rapoport, there is no evidence that drugs were actually taken, with the term 'hashish-eaters' used by orthodox Muslims in reaction to the fact that the Assassins apparently showed no feelings or remorse in carrying out murders. Rapoport, p. 666.
7 Rapoport, p. 659.
8 Quoted in Modern History Sourcebook: Maximilien Robespierre: Justification of the Use of Terror, online at: http://www.fordham.edu/halsall/mod/robespierre-terror.html Downloaded 8 January 2003.
9 Bruce Hoffman, *Inside Terrorism*, Columbia University Press: New York, 1988, p. 17.
10 Walter Laqueur, *The New Terrorism: Fanaticism and the Arms of Mass Destruction*, Oxford University Press: New York, 1999, p. 20.
11 Jessica Stern, *The Ultimate Terrorists*, Cambridge: Harvard University Press, 2001, pp 16-17.
12 See Hoffman, pp. 20-23.
13 Adrian Guelke, *The Age of Terrorism and the International Political System*, I. B. Tauris: New York, 1998, p. 3.
14 Hoffman, p. 25. The opposing arguments in such an approach shall be discussed in a forthcoming article in CDI's *Explaining Terrorism* on defining terrorism.
15 Stern, p. 14.

■ The above information is from The Center for Defense Information's web site which can be found at www.cdi.org
© *The Center for Defense Information*

Methods of attack

Terrorists can murder and maim using many different methods of attack, and we know that as well as using tried and tested methods, Al Qaida and associated groups are able to innovate, as demonstrated on 11 September 2001

The major types of attack which we have seen Al Qaida using are:

Bombs

In vehicles, parcels, on suicide bombers or planted in buildings. While bombs can be detonated remotely, it has become a trademark of Al Qaida to use suicide operatives to ensure a bomb reaches its target. Bombs may be made of commercial or military grade explosives, or home-made materials. They may be large or small, but either way can cause considerable damage both immediately to buildings and bystanders, and longer term to a country's economic interests.

As seen with the 11 September 2001 attacks in the US, Al Qaida has used planes themselves as bombs to attack targets on the ground, by means of hijacking. Other incidents involving airplanes include, in December 2001, Richard Reid's thwarted attempt to bring down an airliner with a small improvised explosive device concealed in his shoes, and an unsuccessful missile attack on an Israeli charter plane departing from Mombasa in November 2002. Al Qaida has also carried out two suicide attacks against ships using explosives packed into small boats (both off the coast of Yemen, in 2000 and 2002).

Recent examples of terrorist bombs include the attacks on the British Consulate and HSBC bank in Istanbul in November 2003, which were suicide attacks using vehicle-borne devices, and the Madrid train bombs in March 2004, where the explosives were left on the trains concealed in bags.

Bombs are Al Qaida's most frequently deployed method of attack.

Shootings

Although targeted assassinations have been less of a feature of recent

international terrorism, the murder of US Aid diplomat Lawrence Foley in Jordan in October 2002 shows the potential for targets to be singled out in this way. There have also been numerous shootings in Saudi Arabia, especially in recent months.

Abductions and kidnappings

Kidnapping has been a favoured tactic of a number of separatist groups, particularly in Asia and South America, to obtain money or in order to apply pressure for a particular political change. The kidnapping of US journalist Daniel Pearl in Pakistan in February 2002 resulted in his murder.

Attacks have also included the use of decapitation and the slitting of victim's throats. This tactic has been used in recent attacks in Saudi Arabia and Iraq.

Chemical, biological and radiological devices

To date, few terrorist attacks have

> *Kidnapping has been a favoured tactic of a number of separatist groups, particularly in Asia and South America*

---

involved CBRN material, and no attacks have taken place in the UK. Alternative methods of attack, such as bombs, are easier, more reliable and safer for terrorists to acquire or use. Nevertheless, it is possible that Al Qaida may seek to use chemical, biological or radiological material against the West. Osama bin Laden has alluded to such devices on several occasions. In November 2001, he said that 'if America used chemical or nuclear weapons against us, then we may retort with chemical and nuclear weapons. We have the weapons as a deterrent'. In a June 2002 article, Al Qaida spokesman Sulaiman Abu Gaith also said 'it is our right to fight [the Americans] with chemical and biological weapons'.

Some of Al Qaida's terrorist attacks overseas are listed on the Foreign and Commonwealth Office website.

In addition to physical attack methods, terrorists may also try to get access to information that may be of use to them, for example by infiltrating an organisation or securing the assistance of an 'insider'.

■ The above information is from MI5's website which can be found at www.MI5.gov.uk

Terrorism: the problems of definition

Information from the Center for Defense Information

By Mark Burgess

Defining terrorism has become so polemical and subjective an undertaking as to resemble an art rather than a science. Texts on the subject proliferate and no standard work on terrorism can be considered complete without at least an introductory chapter being devoted to this issue.[1] Media coverage of terrorist incidents over the years has further confounded the difficulties of defining terrorism, which is variously described as the work of, among others, 'commandos', 'extremists', fundamentalists', and 'guerillas'. As David Rapoport cautioned of this phenomenon almost three decades ago; 'In attempting to correct the abuse of language for political purposes our journalists may succeed in making language altogether useless.'[2] The negative connotations associated with the word 'terrorism' have further complicated attempts to arrive at a subjective definition of the term.

Some experts on terrorism are sceptical as to whether the seemingly interminable attempts to define terrorism are capable of bearing fruit. As, one, Walter Laqueur, opines: 'Even if there were an objective, value-free definition of terrorism,

covering all its important aspects and features, it would still be rejected by some for ideological reasons [...]'[3] This assertion will probably remain true. However, if such a definition is a destination, the journey towards it can almost be an end in itself. Arriving at a working definition also has uses other than increasing our understanding of terrorism. For by defining terrorism one can also define the preferred means of countering it. Defining terrorism also allows terrorists to be defined (or not), justifying (or not) any action that is being taken against them.

Ends

War, according to the Prussian theorist Carl von Clausewitz's famous dictum, is 'the continuation of political intercourse with the addition of other means'[4]. Much the same has been said of terrorism, a violent phenomenon often seen as distinguished partly by its practitioners' political motivations. This view of terrorism as political violence possibly stems from its roots as a

political term applied to the French Revolutionary tribunals active during that country's 'Reign of Terror', with terrorism's political connotations continuing to feature throughout much of its historical development.[5] As one long-time scholar of the phenomenon puts it: 'Terrorism, in the most widely accepted contemporary usage of the term, is fundamentally and inherently political.'[6] However, as with many definitional characteristics of terrorism, this view of it as always being political is not universally accepted. Nor is motivation always considered a factor in deciding what is and is not terrorism.

This was the position of the late Eqbal Ahmad, who argued that motivations 'make no difference'.[7] Jessica Stern agrees, seeing any definition of terrorism as being unlimited by either 'perpetrator or purpose.' This approach, while not excluding political goals as a terrorist aim, also allows for other motivations, such as the purely criminal, or even religious. To Stern it is the 'deliberate evocation of dread is what sets terrorism apart from simple murder or assault.'[8] Such a reading underlay the recent judicial ruling

that the chief suspect in the rash of 'sniper' murders that occurred in the Washington, DC, area last year could be charged under Virginia's new post-Sept. 11, 2001 anti-terrorism law.

The question over whether the snipers should be classified as terrorists, although they clearly did 'terrorise' the DC metropolitan area for a time, highlights the dilemma of broadening the definition of terrorism to include violence that is not primarily political in intent. Such a widening has drawbacks. As a brief survey by one scholar shows, by the 1990s, the word terrorism had been applied to issues as diverse as: Apartheid; 'consumer terrorism' (the poisoning of food products in super-markets by criminal extortionists); 'economic terrorism' (i.e. 'aggressive' currency speculation); 'narco-terrorism'; obscene phone calls; pornography; rape; and, state terror-ism.[9] Such a broad interpretation of terrorism risks making the term so elastic as to deprive it of its meaning.

In addition, the assumption that the psychological effect of terrorism is uppermost in terrorists' minds when they act is also debatable. Often, despite its name, the primary intent of terrorism appears to be to kill rather than frighten. This has been contended to have been the case with the 1998 bombing of an airliner over Lockerbie, with Libyan involvement most likely retaliation for the bombing of that country by the United States in 1986.[10] Certainly, revenge seems to have at least partly provoked the periodic rounds of 'tit for tat' killing that characterised much of Northern Ireland's 'troubles' (although, here, as with Lockerbie, political con-siderations also played a role, with such killings seeking to consolidate loyalist and republican terrorists' self-proclaimed role as protectors of their respective communities). The Sept. 11 attacks on the United States also appear to have been at least partly motivated by revenge (for what the perpetrators viewed as American actions against Muslims), a desire to kill large numbers of people, and the political aspirations of al Qaeda.

Political motivation is persuasively argued by Paul R. Pillar

The negative connotations associated with the word 'terrorism' have further complicated attempts to arrive at a subjective definition of the term

to be a prerequisite of terrorism, although he concedes that criminal activity is not only often undertaken by terrorists, but can often have political repercussions of its own. As Pillar states:

Terrorism is fundamentally different from these other forms of violence, however, in what gives rise to it and in how it must be countered, beyond simple physical security and police techniques. Terrorists' concerns are macro-concerns about changing a larger order; other violent criminals are focused on the micro-level of pecuniary gain and personal relationships. 'Political' in this regard encompasses not just traditional left-right politics but also what are frequently described as religious motivations or social issues.[11]

While terrorism can be identified as political violence, it is far from the case that all political violence can therefore be regarded as terrorism. War, for instance, is a form of political violence, but one which is, generally speaking, differentiated from terrorist action. This trend is partly connected to the tendency to label certain acts of political violence terrorism on the basis of their perpetrator's identity.

Means

Terrorists tend to justify their methods by insisting these are forced upon them due to a lack of resources, and renounce attempts to describe their actions as terrorism. Often, as is the case with the names adopted by such groups, the assertion is made that, rather than terrorists, they are fighters or soldiers in a cause, albeit ones forced by circumstances to use differing strategies, tactics, and

methods from better-equipped national armies. This insistence (which ignores the benefits attached to terrorist methods – unless these are viewed as serendipitous side-effects) extends to terrorists demand-ing that they be treated as prisoners of war and not criminals. The conviction with which this assertion is often held was demonstrated by Provisional Irish Republican Army prisoners in the 1980s when 10 of them died on hunger strikes in protest at the UK government's decision to end their 'special category status' – a move which meant they would now be regarded at criminals rather than the prisoners of war they wished to be regarded as.

However, war is regulated by a series of laws (in theory if not always in fact) that prohibit certain weapons and tactics as well as precluding attacks on certain categories of targets (most notably non-combatants) and placing restrictions on the treatment of prisoners. The terrorist often ignores such laws as are codified in the Geneva Con-ventions, targeting non-combatants, operating in civilian clothes, and taking (and often mistreating or killing) hostages. From that point of view, anyone using such tactics is waging terrorism rather than war. One UN report on the topic takes this further, suggesting that a simplified definition of acts of terrorism could see these as the 'peacetime equivalents of war crimes'.[12] Such an approach not only offers a way of identifying terrorists via their methods, but provides a framework for punitive action against those found guilty of terrorism, offering a potential solution to the controversy this often entails – as evidenced by the current controversy over the status of the suspected terrorists currently being held by the US authorities at Guantanamo Bay.

An emphasis on method over purported aims also tends to make terrorist acts appear less legitimate. In the words of one analyst: 'Cate-gories of ends, such as revolution, coup d'etat, and counter-insurgency, are far less emotive or derogatory than categories of means, such as assassination, bombings, and torture, despite the evident interdependence of means and ends.'[13] Terrorism, as a sort of catch-all for such tactics, is, as seen, a similarly vitriolic term – perhaps even more so. As such it is unsurprising that those who hold that it is the means adopted by terrorists that distinguish them as such tend themselves to identify with the victims of terrorism. Frequently, the advocates of this approach have been on the receiving end of the violence they term terrorism. They also often represent, or belong to, those interests (usually states) which seek to maintain the status quo that the terrorist often seeks to change.[14]

On first appearance, the methods of the terrorist appear almost identical to those of the guerilla, with both bombing civilian areas, carrying out assassinations, and seizing hostages. Moreover, the same intention to influence behaviour through intimidation is also present in both groups. However, guerillas differ from terrorists in that they tend to form larger, more heavily-armed organisations that control territorial zones. While groups will sometimes conduct both guerilla and terrorist campaigns, often simultaneously – such as is currently the case with al Qaeda for instance – terrorism and guerilla warfare are not the same thing.

As this illustrates, while identifying terrorism by the methods used is perhaps the most practical means of arriving at a workable definition of the term, this is only true if general agreement can be reached as to how to differentiate terrorist means from non-terrorist means. Where such terrorist means co-exist with the political motivation discussed above, defining terrorism becomes easier. In addition, while their identity alone is insufficiently subjective a basis to help identify the perpetrators of political violence as terrorists, the identity of their victims – namely their status as 'legitimate' or 'illegitimate targets' – is not. Again, the use of such a determinant is dependent on agreement being reached as to what constitutes a non-combatant in such instances.

None of which is to say that Laqueur's warning on the impossibility of formulating a generally agreed upon definition of terrorism

is likely to become any less true any time soon. However, as argued, this does not necessarily make such a definition – or efforts to arrive at it – any less desirable.

References

1 Most of the texts referred to below include extensive sections which address the issue of defining terrorism, and the reader is referred to these for a more detailed analysis of the problems this entails.
2 David Rapoport, 'The Politics of Atrocity,' in, Yonah Alexander, and Seymour Maxwell Finger (eds.), Terrorism: Interdisciplinary Perspectives (New York: John Jay Press, 1977), p. 46. Quoted in, Bruce Hoffman, Inside Terrorism (Columbia University Press: New York, 1988), p. 37.
3 Walter Laqueur, The Age of Terrorism (Boston: Little, Brown and Company, 1987). pp. 149-150.
4 Carl von Clausewitz, On War, edited and translated by Michael Howard, and Peter Paret, (Princeton: Princeton University Press, 1989), p. 605.
5 See Mark Burgess, A Brief History of Terrorism, (Washington DC: Center for Defense Information, 2003) for more on the historical development of terrorism.
6 Hoffman, p. 14.
7 Eqbal Ahmad, 'Terrorism: Theirs & Ours,' in Russell D. Howard, and Reid L. Sawyer, Terrorism and Counterterrorism: Understanding the New Security Environment (Guilford: McGraw-Hill/ Dushkin, 2003), pp. 46-53, p. 50.
8 Jessica Stern, The Ultimate Terrorists (Harvard University Press, 1999), p.11.
9 Adrian Guelke, The Age of Terrorism and the International Political System (New York: I. B. Tauris, 1998), p. 1.
10 Guelke, p.5.
11 Paul R. Pillar, Terrorism and US Foreign Policy (Brookings Institution Press, 2001), pp. 13-14.
12 United Nations Office on Drugs and Crime, Definitions of Terrorism, online at: http://www.unodc.org/unodc/terrorism_definitions.html Downloaded, 7/28/03.
13 Guelke, p. 28.
14 Clearly this is not universally the case. For instance loyalist terrorist groups in Northern Ireland could be argued to have begun life with the intent of defending the status quo.

■ The above information is from the Center for Defense Information's website which can be found at www.cdi.org

---

While terrorism can be identified as political violence, it is far from the case that all political violence can therefore be regarded as terrorism

The war against terrorism

Living with fear and uncertainty in a changing world of terrorism

Never before have five men armed with razor blades and pocket knives demonstrated such power. Never before have ordinary men and women realised just how easy it is for a single act of terrorism to destroy the confidence of a nation as well as the corner of a great city. And confidence is everything. The terrorist events themselves in biological terms were pin-pricks – with very few deaths in relation to the entire population of America. But the psychological impact of terrorism on that day will be felt for more than a generation.

Take air travel for example:

It is right to be sober. Every act of terrorism for the next hundred years will be measured by terrorists themselves against this new yardstick of terrible 'success'.

International terrorism

Expect plenty more attacks by hundreds of different groups campaigning on different issues – despite every effort of governments around the world to prevent terrorism. Expect an intense effort by ambitious terrorists to beat recent Hollywood-style disaster images with something even more dramatic, more awful, more panic-inducing. The power of terrorism comes from fear of the unseen as well as the seen. A mighty act which also perhaps unleashes biological weapons, bacteria, or viruses or radiation.

Fear is the greatest weakness of the 'free' Western world, in a media-dominated age where people no longer trust government experts nor scientists. Scare stories of terrorism travel fast and inflame the mind.

As I wrote in the first edition of *Futurewise*, Tribalism feeds terrorism. Tribalism is the most powerful force on earth, more powerful than all the atomic bombs on earth, the US, Russian and Chinese armies combined. What happened at the World Trade Towers is unfortunately only one expression of a wider and

Dr Patrick Dixon

deeper tribalism which will continue to impact the lives of billions of people over the next twenty years.

The roots of terrorism were sown long in the past and the branches will dominate our future.

Tribalism is intimately connected with terrorism: when one mass of people identify only with themselves and their values, and see others as lesser beings, then the ground is set for permanent conflict.

Most wars for the last twenty years have been wars inside nations rather than between them: wars over culture and ideology, conflicts that affect tribal groups and loyalties rather than national boundaries and identity, where one or both sides often resort to terrorism. Expect that pattern to continue regardless of the response the US and other countries make to recent events, and the inevitable counter-reactions that are provoked.

The lesson of history shows that counter terrorism requires more than military action and intelligence gathering.

It's incorrect to say that Islamic Fundamentalism is the root of the global terrorism threat. The truth is that the forces and causes of terrorism are far more diverse. The fact is that there are hundreds of small to large groups today who use random attacks on civilian and commercial targets as a means of getting attention and winning support (they hope). Take the patterns of terrorism in Chechnya, Kosovo, Bosnia, Northern Ireland, the Basque separatists and

> *The roots of terrorism were sown long in the past and the branches will dominate our future*

more recent rioting in anti-globalisation protests. It's just the start.

If terrorism thrives on tribalism, then a sense of injustice is what feeds tribalism. When a group feels they are marginalised, their power destroyed, their people victimised, their voices unheard, then violent protests are sure to follow.

The trouble is that there has never been a time in human history when so many millions have felt 'just' grievances. One such issue is the growing gulf between the rich and the poor, the destitute and the power-players. Another is the claim by the United Nations that sanctions against Iraq have resulted in the deaths of over 500,000 children. Another is the desperate situation of millions of near-starving people in Africa and Asia who see their super-rich global villagers on CNN every day.

Attacks and raids on the Taliban in Afghanistan, biological warfare retaliation by terrorists (anthrax at first) that may or may not be associated with Osama bin Laden, other terrorist acts – it is easy to set up a cycle of low grade conflict as we have seen in many parts of the world. These cycles of terrorism can fuel acts of violence for generations and are difficult to stop.

The new world order will have to address all these fundamental global challenges, as well as issues of security.

In the meantime, expect ethics and values to become ever more important to every company, large corporation, organisation, politician and people group.

Never has it been more important for the whole of humanity together to agree how we can build a better kind of world.

■ Article written by Dr Patrick Dixon in 2003, Chairman Global Change Ltd, author of *Futurewise* – see www.globalchange.com/main.htm for 30,000 pages and 50 videos by Dr Dixon on future trends.

The unrealistic war on terror

Information from *The Muslim News*

September 2004 marked the third anniversary of 9/11. It also saw the massacre of more than 300 school children, teachers and parents in the North Ossetian town of Belsam – a tragedy compounded by the chaos and incompetence of the Russian security services. There was also a car bomb outside the Australian Embassy in Indonesia that killed nine people and injured more than 180. Whether in Spain, South Korea, Nepal or elsewhere in the world, all attacks are being tarnished with the same brush of 'international terrorism', regardless of their cause.

In Iraq and Afghanistan, there is even a more incessant use of violence that is being erroneously branded as being the centre of the 'war on terror'. Whilst it may have been a travesty to assert that the events of 9/11 were the worst crime in recent history merely because they took place on American soil, it was even a bigger blunder by the US and its allies to declare a so-called war that creates an unrealistic public perception of the dilemma. It not only creates a psychosis of fear that is used to build bigger barriers and more draconian laws but also implies that some kind of 'victory' can be achieved on the battleground that has neither borders nor boundaries. There is no identifiable enemy other than al-Qaida, an all-embracing term that is abused to wilfully and deceitfully present terrorism as a specifically Muslim problem associated with the mis-interpretation of Islam.

The central issue is that no debate has been allowed to consider the cause of the latest wave of terrorism. The term itself was first used in Europe two centuries ago by the French revolutionaries, in an exact reverse of the contemporary sense – to denote state violence against a people. It only came to the Middle East after its use by the Zionist Irgun against the Palestinians in its campaign to establish an Israeli state. An analysis in August 2004 by Justin Lewis from the Cardiff School of Journalism, Media and Cultural Studies, found that the number of incidents and victims of terrorist was at its lowest for years and that the actual levels of risks do not equate with the saturation media coverage since 9/11. He suggested that it was rather an increase in political rhetoric.

The central issue is that no debate has been allowed to consider the cause of the latest wave of terrorism

---

Since declaring his dubious war, Bush ushered in a new era of geopolitics, defined by pre-emptive wars and attacks on terrorist infra-structures under the guise that it can be resolved by military means. In the process, it has led to the profiling of Muslims worldwide. Yet, as exampled in Iraq, the war has only exacerbated the situation as it is widely recognised that there were no so-called anti-western terrorists before the invasion and occupation. Missing has been any attempt to address the causes and make real aspirations to equality and mutual respect.

However outrageous the mind-less child killing in Beslan, Russian President Vladimir Putin has made the same mistakes by following the Bush doctrine and presenting the Chechen conflict as a problem of international terrorism that seemingly started only after 9/11 and not decades ago. The biggest example of setting such rules has been Israel in the deceitful battle of good against evil. Yet the daily atrocities committed by Israel are systematically ignored in the west. There can be no answer to terrorist threats without addressing the causes as has been shown in Northern Ireland. Certainly, practical steps to make progress in conflicts in various part of the world will bring about a more safer world.

■ The above information is from *The Muslim News*' website which can be found at www.muslimnews.co.uk

© The Muslim News

Terrorists and suicide attacks

Information from the Congressional Research Service

Definitions

Some argue that the language used to describe terrorism plays a role in how it is perceived, so words used in describing it must be very carefully chosen. For example, there are many phrases used to describe the phenomenon to be discussed here. Some people use the phrase 'suicide bombings', but that is too restrictive for this report, as it seems to refer only to attacks that are carried out with the use of explosives. Suicide attacks can occur with other types of weapons, including jetliners. 'Genocide bombings' and 'homicide attacks' are phrases frequently used by those who identify with the unwilling victims of attacks; these terms emphasise the criminal nature of the violence and de-emphasise the self-inflicted death of the perpetrator. On the other hand, 'martyrdom operations' places the emphasis upon the cause of the perpetrators, implying a connection to the notions of 'holy war' and/or self defence, even in the killing of civilians.[1] Finally 'suicide operations' places the emphasis on the organisation's role in staging the episodes, implying a military-type character to them.

None of the currently used terms is perfect. For the purposes of this report, the phrase used will be 'suicide attacks', by which is meant, in the sense used here, events where the 'success' of the operation cannot occur without the death of the perpetrator, and he or she is apparently aware of this in advance.[2] Likewise, this report concentrates on suicide attacks that are carried out by 'terrorists', by which is meant nonstate actors whose goal is the threat or use of violence for political ends against noncombatant or civilian targets.[3] These are off-the-battlefield episodes, with the attackers not integrated into units in a formal military sense. Therefore, specifically excluded are high risk military operations, where, although the perpetrator may expect his chances of survival to be virtually nil, he or she is not deliberately seeking his or her own death. And this report also does not include self-inflicted deaths that occur without any violence directed outward, like hunger strikes or cult suicides.[4]

Why would anyone choose to engage in such an attack? The answer to this question requires an insight into the psychological and cultural aspects of terrorism

---

Personal motivations for suicide attacks

One perception about suicide attacks is that they are carried out by individual deranged fanatics but this is almost never the case. Research on suicide attacks indicates that most terrorist operatives are psychologically normal, in the sense that psychological pathology does not seem to be present, and the attacks are virtually always premeditated.[5] There have been instances of

coercion or deception in recruiting suicide attackers and/or executing the attacks,[6] but most perpetrators are as aware of their imminent fate as they are of the fate of their victims.

Why would anyone choose to engage in such an attack? The answer to this question requires an insight into the psychological and cultural aspects of terrorism. The motivations for suicide attacks are not so different in many ways from the motivations for other types of terrorism, including attention to a cause, personal notoriety, anger, revenge and retribution against a perceived injustice.[7] From the perspective of the individual attacker, the act of 'martyrdom' may offer an opportunity to impress an audience and be remembered, an act that may be a powerful incentive for individuals who perceive their lives as having little significance otherwise.[8] Suicide attackers are sometimes widows or bereaved siblings who wish to take vengeance for their loved one's violent death. In the case of widows, for example, the death of the spouse may cut the woman off from productive society and/or leave her with a sense of hopelessness, especially in very traditional societies. Increasing numbers of women seem to be carrying out suicide attacks in recent years, a development that may be partly traced to this factor and will be discussed further below.

A longing for religious purity and/or a strong commitment to the welfare of the group may drive individuals to engage in suicide attacks. The role of the central religious, political, or ethnic culture or ideology is important. Suicide attacks among Palestinian groups, for example, seem to have inspired a self-perpetuating subculture of martyrdom.[9] Children who grow up in such settings may be subtly indoctrinated in a culture glorifying ultimate sacrifice in the service of the Palestinian cause and against the Israeli people. There are social, cultural, religious, and material incentives presented in such a context, sometimes including spiritual rewards in the after life, vast celebrity, cash bonuses, free apartments and/or the guarantee of a place with God for the attackers' families.

Other attackers seem to be driven apparently by a sense of humiliation or injustice, a worrisome development that has appeared for example among young Egyptians.[10] Some argue, for example, that perceptions regarding the plight of the Palestinian people may have had an influence upon the willingness of young Egyptians to participate in suicide attacks, especially among those who are unemployed and frustrated for other reasons.[11] Indeed, desperation is often mentioned in press reports: Palestinians in particular are quoted as saying that suicide attacks are the 'weapon of last resort'.[12]

In some conflicts, increasing use of suicide attacks is seen widely as a potential sign that the struggle is being 'Islamicised'. The historical connection to the Muslim Assassins groups is often mentioned. Al Qaeda's use of suicide attacks is well known, and growing links between that organisation and many other, more local indigenous groups are sometimes demonstrated at least in part by a shift in the local group's tactics.[13] For example, the recent use of suicide attacks by Chechen militants is seen by some as a worrisome indicator of growing influence of radical Islamist factions within Chechnya and/or links with radical groups like Al Qaeda.[14] Recent suicide attacks in Morocco are likewise viewed this way.[15] The August 2003 suicide attacks on the Jordanian Embassy and the UN Headquarters in Iraq may also reflect a shift from local nationalistic resistance to the more active involvement of outside Islamist fighters.

So-called 'martyrdom' is not just a religious concept, however. The tradition of heroic martyrdom, where

the hero sacrifices to save the life of his community, nation, or people, is a powerful element in many secular traditions. Among Palestinian groups non-religious nationalist motivations are sometimes dominant, especially with respect to groups such as the al-Aqsa Martyrs' Brigades, which is an offshoot of militant elements of the essentially secular PLO's Fatah faction. Indeed, globally, an apparently larger proportion overall of the suicide attacks of the last twenty years has been carried out by secular groups like the Tamil Tigers and the PKK, who both appeal primarily to traditional concepts of nationhood and sacrifice, than by religiously-motivated groups.

Following the September 11th attacks, one of the important developments among those who study terrorism has been the re-examination of the concept of a 'profile' or typical characteristics of suicide attackers.[16] Some people had argued on the basis of research done especially on Hamas members, that suicide terrorists were typically male, aged 18-27 years, unmarried, relatively uneducated, and highly susceptible to suggestion.[17] This

description proved to be inadequate, however, especially after the 9/11 attacks in which older, well-educated operatives like Mohammed Atta participated. In the Palestinian intifada, as well, previous assumptions are being reexamined, with suicide attacks being carried out by operatives as diverse as a college student, a middle-aged married man with children, and the son of a wealthy businessman, not to mention increasing numbers of women and children.[18] Some have argued that there is no pattern to these 'profiles' at all.[19] In any case, as we move into the twenty-first century, stereotypes about who is likely to carry out terrorist suicide attacks are evaporating.

Although research indicates that individual suicide attackers make choices and are not technically 'crazy', according to experts they are often manipulated by the pressures and belief structures of the group.[20] Because of this, it is important to study the role of the organization in the phenomenon.

References

1   Haim Malka, 'Must Innocents Die? The Islamic Debate over Suicide Attacks,' *Middle East Quarterly* (Spring 2003), p. 26.

2   Ibid. See also Scott Atran, 'Genesis of Suicide Terrorism,' *Science*, 7 March 2003, Vol. 299, p. 1534.

3   The question of a definition of terrorism is much-debated, but the central elements of the concept are generally agreed. For more information, see Audrey Kurth Cronin, 'Behind the Curve:

A longing for religious purity and/or a strong commitment to the welfare of the group may drive individuals to engage in suicide attacks

---

Globalization and International Terrorism,' *International Security*, Vol. 27, No. 3 (Winter 2002/03), pp. 32-33. On the challenges of defining terrorism, see also Omar Malik, *Enough of the Definition of Terrorism!* Royal Institute of International Affairs (London: RIIA, 2001); and Alex P. Schmid, *Political Terrorism: A Research Guide* (New Brunswick, NJ: Transaction Books, 1984).

4 Yoram Schweitzer, 'Suicide Terrorism: Development and main characteristics,' in *Countering Suicide Terrorism: An International Conference* (Herzliya, Israel: the International Policy Institute for Counter-Terrorism, 2001), pp. 75-76.

5 Jerrold Post, 'The Mind of the Terrorist: Individual and Group Psychology of Terrorist Behavior,' testimony prepared for the Subcommittee on Emerging Threats and Capabilities, Senate Armed Service Committee, 15 November 2001; and Ehud Sprinzak, 'Rational Fanatics,' *Foreign Policy*, September/October 2000, pp. 66-73.

6 See, for example, the PKK, below.

7 Crenshaw, p.25

8 Ibid., p. 26.

9 David Brooks, 'The Culture of Martyrdom,' *Atlantic Monthly*, Vol. 289, No. 6 (June 2002), pp. 18-20.

10 Tim Golden, 'Young Egyptians Hearing Calls of Martyrdom For Palestinian Cause ,' *The New York Times International*, 26 April 2002, p. A1.

11 Ibid.

12 Daniel Williams, 'Where Palestinian martyrs Are Groomed; West Bank City of Jenin Emerges as Suicide Bomb Capital,' *The Washington Post*, 15 August 2001, p. A1.

13 For more on the evolution of Al Qaeda's tactics and organisation, see CRS Report RS21529, *Al Qaeda after the Iraq Conflict.*

14 Reuven Paz, 'Suicide Terrorist Operations in Chechnya: An Escalation of the Islamist Struggle,' International Policy Institute for Counterterrorism, accessed at [http://www.ict.org.il] on 10 July 2003; and Nabi Abdullaev, 'Suicide Attacks Take Rebel Fight to a New Level,' *The Moscow Times*, 16 May 2003, p. 3; accessed at [http://www.themoscowtimes.com] on 17 July 2003.

15 See CRS Report RS21579, *Morocco: Current Issues.*

16 For a survey of previous research on terrorist profiling, see Rex A. Hudson, *Who Becomes a Terrorist and Why: The 1999 Government Report on Profiling Terrorists* (Guilford, Connecticut: The Lyons Press, [2001]), especially pp. 67-108.

17 See, for example, Boaz Ganor, Executive Director, International Policy Institute for Counter-Terrorism, 'Suicide Terrorism: an Overview, Who is the shahid? p. 3, 15 February 2000 [http://www.ict.org.il/articles/articledet.cfrm? articleid=128] accessed on 27 July 2001.

18 Rebecca Trounson and Tracy Wilkinson, 'Analysts Rethink Image of Suicide Bombers,' *The Los Angeles Times*, 20 September 2001; accessed at [http://www.latimes.com] on 22 July 2003.

19 James Bennet, 'Rash of New Suicide Bombers Exhibit No Patterns or Ties,' , 21 June 2002, p. A1.

20 Post testimony, Subcommittee on Emerging Threats and Capabilities, Senate Armed Service Committee, 15 November 2001.

© *Congressional Research Service*

Think again: Al Qaeda

The mere mention of al Qaeda conjures images of an efficient terrorist network guided by a powerful criminal mastermind. Yet al Qaeda is more lethal as an ideology than as an organisation. 'Al Qaedaism' will continue to attract supporters in the years to come – whether Osama bin Laden is around to lead them or not.

'Al Qaeda is a global terrorist organisation'
No. It is less an organisation than an ideology. The Arabic word *qaeda* can be translated as a 'base of operation' or 'foundation', or alternatively as a 'precept' or 'method'. Islamic militants always understood the term in the latter sense. In 1987, Abdullah Azzam, the leading ideologue for modern Sunni Muslim radical activists, called for al-qaeda al-sulbah (a vanguard of the strong). He envisaged men who, acting independently, would set an example for the rest of the Islamic world and

By Jason Burke

thus galvanise the *umma* (global community of believers) against its oppressors. It was the FBI – during its investigation of the 1998 US Embassy bombings in East Africa – which dubbed the loosely linked group of activists that Osama bin Laden and his aides had formed as 'al Qaeda'. This decision was partly due to institutional conservatism and partly because the FBI had to apply conventional antiterrorism laws to

an adversary that was in no sense a traditional terrorist or criminal organisation.

Although bin Laden and his partners were able to create a structure in Afghanistan that attracted new recruits and forged links among preexisting Islamic militant groups, they never created a coherent terrorist network in the way commonly conceived. Instead, al Qaeda functioned like a venture capital firm – providing funding, contacts, and expert advice to many different militant groups and individuals from all over the Islamic world.

Today, the structure that was built in Afghanistan has been destroyed, and bin Laden and his associates have scattered or been arrested or killed. There is no longer a central hub for Islamic militancy. But the al Qaeda worldview, or 'al Qaedaism', is growing stronger every day. This radical internationalist ideology – sustained by anti-Western, anti-Zionist, and anti-Semitic rhetoric – has adherents among many individuals and groups, few of whom are currently linked in any substantial way to bin Laden or those around him. They merely follow his precepts, models, and methods. They act in the style of al Qaeda, but they are only part of al Qaeda in the very loosest sense. That's why Israeli intelligence services now prefer the term 'jihadi international' instead of 'al Qaeda'.

'Capturing or killing bin Laden will deal a severe blow to al Qaeda'

Wrong. Even for militants with identifiable ties to bin Laden, the death of the 'sheik' will make little difference in their ability to recruit people. US Secretary of Defense Donald Rumsfeld recently acknowledged as much when he questioned in an internal Pentagon memo whether it was possible to kill militants faster than radical clerics and religious schools could create them. In practical terms, bin Laden now has only a very limited ability to commission acts of terror, and his

---

There is no longer a central hub for Islamic militancy. But the al Qaeda worldview, or 'al Qaedaism', is growing stronger every day

---

involvement is restricted to the broad strategic direction of largely autonomous cells and groups. Most intelligence analysts now consider him largely peripheral.

This turn of events should surprise no one. Islamic militancy predates bin Laden's activities. He was barely involved in the Islamic violence of the early 1990s in Algeria, Egypt, Bosnia, and Kashmir. His links to the 1993 World Trade Center attack were tangential. There were no al Qaeda training camps during the early 1990s, although camps run by other groups churned out thousands of highly trained fanatics. Even when bin Laden was based in Afghanistan in the late 1990s, it was often Islamic groups and individuals who sought him out for help in finding resources for preconceived attacks, not vice versa. These days, Islamic groups can go to other individuals, such as Jordanian activist Abu Musab al-Zarqawi, who set up his al Tauhid group in competition with bin Laden (rather than, as is

frequently claimed, in alliance with him) to obtain funds, expertise, or other logistical assistance.

Bin Laden still plays a significant role in the movement as a propagandist who effectively exploits modern mass communications. It is likely that the United States will eventually apprehend bin Laden and that this demonstration of US power will demoralise many militants. However, much depends on the manner in which he is captured or killed. If, like deposed Iraqi President Saddam Hussein, he surrenders without a fight, which is very unlikely, many followers will be deeply disillusioned. If he achieves martyrdom in a way that his cohorts can spin as heroic, he will be an inspiration for generations to come. Either way, bin Laden's removal from the scene will not stop Islamic militancy.

'The militants seek to destroy the West so they can impose a global Islamic state'

False. Islamic militants' main objective is not conquest, but to beat back what they perceive as an aggressive West that is supposedly trying to complete the project begun during the Crusades and colonial periods of denigrating, dividing, and humiliating Islam. The militants' secondary goal is the establishment of the caliphate, or single Islamic state, in the lands roughly corresponding to the furthest extent of the Islamic empire of the late first and early second centuries. Today, this state would encompass the Middle East, the Maghreb (North Africa bordering the Mediterranean), Andalusia in southern Spain, Central Asia, parts of the Balkans, and possibly some Islamic territories in the Far East. Precisely how this utopian caliphate would function is vague. The militants believe that if all Muslims act according to a literal interpretation of the Islamic holy texts, an almost mystical transformation to a just and perfect society will follow.

■ The above information is from Foreign Policy's website which can be found at www.foreignpolicy.com

The European Union response to terrorism

Information from the Anti-Defamation League

When Islamic extremist terrorism hit European soil with the March 2004 Madrid rail bombings, a new sense of urgency prompted greater Europe-wide cooperative counterterrorism efforts.

The European Union in fact had already begun to tackle seriously the issue of international terrorism after the September 11th World Trade Center attacks and passed several significant anti-terrorism measures. Many of these new provisions, however, were not implemented by individual EU nations. Meanwhile, the ongoing discovery of diffuse and multilayered Al Qaeda and Al Qaeda-linked terror cells across Europe made enhanced intra-European and European-US cooperation an increasing necessity.

The recently expanded 25-nation European Union faces formidable challenges on the counter-terrorism front. The porous borders among EU member states, for example, impede law enforcement authorities trying to halt terrorist goods across Europe. In addition, political issues and the practical problems of diverse legal and bureaucratic regulations and differing languages and cultures make it difficult for the EU to streamline the law enforcement and domestic and foreign intelligence agencies of all member states into an efficient, cohesive and effective counterterrorist instrument.

Counterterrorism post-September 11th

Following September 11th, the EU took a number of steps to increase its counterterrorism capabilities. Most significantly, the EU adopted a common definition of terrorism, a European Arrest Warrant and a list of terrorist organisations.

The EU 'Council Framework Decision of 13 June 2002 on combating terrorism' seeks to ensure that the definition of terrorist crimes is similar across the Union and sets common minimum and maximum penalties for terrorist crimes. Before the framework decision was adopted, only seven EU countries had specific laws to fight terrorism and those laws varied from country to country.

According to the framework, a 'terrorist act' is one that 'may seriously damage a country or an international organisation' when the objective is: '(1) seriously intimidating a population, or (2) unduly compelling a Government or international organisation to perform or abstain from performing any act, or (3) seriously destabilising or destroying the fundamental political, constitutional, economic or social structures of a country or international organisation.'

Acts that are deemed terrorist offences include: killing and wounding people, kidnapping, hostage-taking, attacks on government and public facilities and infrastructure, hijacking aircraft, ships or other means of public or goods transport, acquiring or using explosives or weapons of mass destruction, interfering with fundamental natural resources, and threatening to commit any of the above acts. Directing a terrorist group and participating in the activities of a terrorist group 'with knowledge of the fact that such participation will contribute to the criminal activities of the group' are also punishable offences.

The European Arrest Warrant provides for simplified surrender procedures between judicial authorities of member states, based upon the principle of mutual recognition of judicial decisions. An arrest warrant issued in one country is now valid in all other EU nations. The measure was adopted in order to ensure that individuals wanted for terrorism in one country could not continue to operate in other European countries.

Regarding terrorist organisations, at this writing, the EU has a list of 25 designated foreign terrorist organisations. Member states are required to freeze assets of the organisations and members of the banned groups are subject to prosecution on terrorism charges. The list includes several Palestinian groups, Greek organisations, Irish groups, and the Basque separatist group ETA. Recent additions to the list include the political wing of

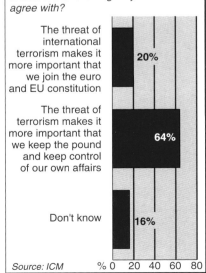

Terrorism and the EU

ICM Research interviewed a random sample of 1021 adults aged 18+ by telephone on 24-25 March 2004. Interviews were conducted across the country and the results have been weighted to the profile of all adults.

Which of the following do you more agree with?

The threat of international terrorism makes it more important that we join the euro and EU constitution — 20%

The threat of terrorism makes it more important that we keep the pound and keep control of our own affairs — 64%

Don't know — 16%

Source: ICM   % 0 20 40 60 80

Hamas and Colombia's National Liberation Army (ELN). Noticeably absent from the list of terrorist organisations is the south Lebanon-based Hezbollah.

In the area of law enforcement cooperation, the EU created joint police investigation teams across the bloc, a special Europol (Europe's police agency) anti-terrorism unit charged with collecting, sharing and analysing information concerning international terrorism and Eurojust, a coordinating body between member states' law enforcement agencies. The EU's Terrorist Working Group (TWG) assesses the terrorist threat every six months, keeps an updated common list identifying the most significant terrorist organisations, and defines new cooperation instruments. The EU Police Chiefs Task Force and the heads of the EU Counter Terrorist Units meet regularly to exchange information and experiences.

Counterterrorism post-Madrid

Following the Madrid attacks, the European Commission issued an 'action paper in response to the terrorist attacks on Madrid'. The paper included a 'Declaration on Solidarity Against Terrorism', and called for 'Better implementation of existing legislative instruments relevant to the fight against terrorism, and adoption of draft measures already on the Council table, strengthening the fight against terrorist financing, and enhanced operational coordination and co-operation.'

The solidarity declaration calls on member states to act jointly if a member state is the victim of a terrorist attack. It states that the 'Union shall mobilise all the instruments at its disposal to: prevent the terrorist threat in the territory of the Member States; protect democratic institutions and the civilian population from any terrorist attack; assist a Member State in its territory at the request of its political authorities in the event of a terrorist attack.'

The US and Europe share a commitment to combating international terrorism

---

Regarding implementation of existing legislative instruments, the Commission urged those EU members who have not yet incorporated the European Arrest Warrant into their national law to do so; it called on those states that have not yet fully reported on the implementation of the Framework Decision on the fight against terrorism to do so; called on member states to provide completed information regarding steps taken to identify, trace, freeze and seize terrorist funds; called on member states to notify measures taken to implement joint investigation teams, and other specific measures for police and judicial cooperation; and to implement

existing legislation on maritime and aviation security.

Regarding draft measures already on the Council table, the Commission called for the adoption of the Draft Framework Decisions on the confiscation of crime-related proceeds, instrumentalities and property; on attacks against information systems; and on the European Evidence Warrant. The Commission said that it would soon initiate legislation on cross-border hot pursuit. Regarding measures to strengthen legislation controls on terrorist financing, the Commission called on member states to make the list of designated terrorist organisations operational and 'reactive on a real time basis'. In order to facilitate the application of freezing measures decided by the Union, an electronic database of all targeted persons and entities will be operational in the summer of 2004. The Commission also announced that it will soon propose the establishment of a European Register on convictions – a database of persons, groups and entities covered by restrictive measures for the fight against terrorism or under criminal proceedings for terrorist offences and systems – thus allowing holders of bank accounts to be identified.

In the area of enhancing operational coordination and cooperation, the Commission proposed the following:

■ the creation of a new coordination mechanism for the exchange of information where law enforcement, judicial

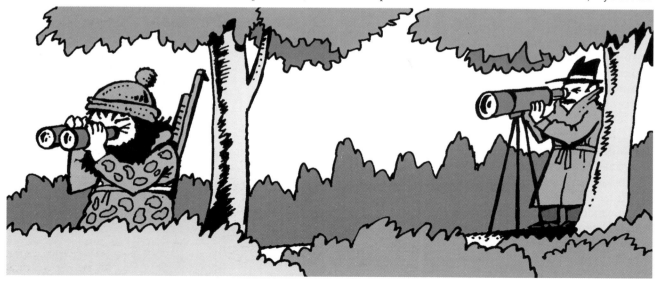

authorities and intelligence services would meet to enhance mutual trust and exchange operational intelligence

- discussions and a proposal outlining an EU approach to the use of travellers' data for border and aviation security and other law enforcement purposes
- comprehensive and interoperable European Information Systems, traceability and control of the weapons of terror and precursors
- strengthening the identification, control and interception of illegal trafficking in materials of weapons of mass destruction
- ratification of the Protocol to the United Nations Transnational Organised Crime Convention on trafficking of illegal firearms
- the consideration of mandatory fingerprinting on EU passports, identity cards and other travel documents
- strengthening Europol, Eurojust and the Task Force of EU Police Chiefs

The EU also created the position of a European Counterterrorism Coordinator and appointed former Dutch deputy interior minister Gijs de Vries to fill the post. The coordinator is charged with presenting proposals aimed at better organizing and streamlining the work of the EU secretariat on the fight against terrorism; preparing proposals for better coordination among specialist EU councils and preparatory bodies on security issues; and maintaining regular contacts with member states to ensure the best coordination between EU and national action.

The reaction in Europe to the creation of this new post has been mixed, with many observers citing the potential for ineffectiveness if the coordinator does not receive the full support of all EU member states and the necessary financial and intelligence resources to fulfil his responsibilities. US–European Cooperation

The US and Europe share a commitment to combating international terrorism. In recent testimony before the Senate Foreign Relations Committee's Sub-committee on European Affairs, State

America and Europe: differing approaches toward counterterrorism

As discussed above, there is a great deal of significant and ongoing transatlantic counterterrorist cooperation. On the other hand, the US and Europe do have differing outlooks and approaches toward combating the terrorist threat. Depending on the context and circumstances, these differences have impeded and may continue to hinder various aspects of American-European cooperation.

First, Europe views terrorism primarily as a law enforcement issue, whereas the US views it as a military issue as well. Europeans do not generally see military action as the most effective tool in fighting terror. A European official in Washington was recently quoted as saying: 'We have always had a different definition of terrorism, in that we never call it a "war" on terrorism. We call it the fight or battle against terrorism, and we do think the distinction makes a difference.'

Secondly, Europeans tend to view terrorism as a problem with 'root causes' that need to be addressed. In the European worldview, poverty, inequality, and the Arab-Israeli conflict fuel suicide bombings and other forms of terrorist violence. Along these lines, the EU had refused to list the political wing of Hamas on its list of banned terrorist organisations arguing that Hamas' military and political wings could be separated, the political wing funds vital social services for Palestinians, and that the political wing could potentially play a role in Middle East peace efforts. In September 2003, several weeks after a Hamas suicide bombing in Jerusalem killed 23 people, the EU acknowledged the connection between Hamas' military and political wings and listed Hamas as a terrorist organisation.

Thirdly, the European Union believes that governmental action against international terrorism requires the legitimacy of a multilateral framework and thus tends to look more to the United Nations and other international and regional bodies for leadership on this front than would the US.

Department Counterterrorism coordinator Ambassador J. Cofer Black said, 'Europeans have been reliable partners, both bilaterally and in multilateral organisations. Cooperation has been forthcoming, and rapid response to immediate threats the norm.' In the wake of both September 11th and March 11th, the US-EU political dialogue on the issue of terrorism deepened with European and American officials meeting regularly to share intelligence and other information and find ways to enhance anti-terrorist cooperation.

On the concrete level, the US and Europol have concluded several cooperation agreements that enable the exchange of data on terrorism and terrorists between law enforcement authorities. In June 2003, at the US-EU Summit in Washington, Extradition and Mutual Legal Assistance Agreements were signed, expanding law enforcement and judicial cooperation. In April 2004, the EU and the Department of Homeland Security signed an agreement calling for the prompt expansion of the Container Security Initiative (CSI) throughout Europe, thus enhancing efforts to prevent terrorists from exploiting the international trading system. The agreement will also intensify and broaden Customs cooperation and mutual assistance in customs matters between the two blocs.

- The above information is from the Anti-Defamation League's website: www.adl.org

© Reprinted with permission of the Anti-Defamation League

Targeting terrorist funds

Cutting terrorists off from their funds

It does not take much money to fund a terrorist attack, and terrorists are always looking for new ways to obtain and transfer funds. The effort to disrupt the flow of money to terrorists, both at home and internationally, is an important element of counter-terrorism.

Since the September 11 attacks in the US, we have comprehensively overhauled our strategy and practice in this area. Among other measures, we have strengthened our legislation, and developed new multi-agency structures.

What we've achieved so far:

- Numerous terrorist operations have been disrupted.
- Large amounts of cash have been seized under counter-terrorist legislation and frozen under international obligations.
- The UK has fully implemented key anti-terrorist resolutions from the United Nations Security Council, which require all states to freeze terrorist finances. Since the September 11 attacks, over 160 countries and jurisdictions have taken concrete action to freeze terrorist assets, and US$112 million has been frozen worldwide.
- In the UK, both before and since September 11, we have frozen the assets of over 100 organisations and over 200 individuals, totalling some US$100 million. The bulk of these assets have now been unfrozen and made available to the current Government of Afghanistan. Around US $500,000 of terrorist assets remain frozen in the UK.

Making the UK a hostile environment for terrorists

- We will continue to track, freeze and disrupt terrorist money flows, and we will use intelligence gained from terrorist finance investigations to help develop valuable insights into the methodology of terrorist operations.
- We will also continue to lead the way internationally with our financial services industry

---

The UK has fully implemented key anti-terrorist resolutions from the United Nations Security Council, which require all states to freeze terrorist finances

---

outreach programme, which allows government, law enforcement agencies, prominent trade and industry bodies, and regulators to engage quickly and coherently on counter-terrorist finance issues.

The co-operation of the private sector is vital in disrupting and combating terrorist financing, and we are particularly grateful for the wholehearted support of the financial services industry.

Recovering the proceeds of crime

Terrorists also make money through organised crime. We have recently introduced tough new powers for police and customs officers to investigate and seize the money that criminals make from, and intend to use, in crime.

These are the first of the new provisions to be implemented under the Proceeds of Crime Act 2002. The powers are applicable to the proceeds of all crime, not just terrorism.

- The above information is from the Home Office's website which can be found at www.homeoffice.gov.uk

© Crown copyright

TERRORISTS' MILLIONS SEIZED

At the service of politicians

Media coverage of terrorism has ballooned since 9/11, despite the fact that the number of incidents and victims is the lowest for years

By Justin Lewis

The millennium may not be very old, but there's no doubt which news story has dominated it thus far. Since the attacks on the twin towers on September 11 2001, terrorism has remained at the top of the news agenda. Whether it is terrorist incidents, arrests, warnings from politicians or coverage of the actions carried out in the name of the 'war on terror', we have seen more sustained coverage of the issue than at any other time in the modern era.

This is true even if we exclude the peak year of 2001. Since January 2002, the *Times, Financial Times*, the *Guardian*, the *Mail* and the *Mirror*, have, between them, run an average of 400 stories about international terrorism every year. And the trend is upward, not downward. If we compare that with a four-and-a-half-year period before 9/11 (from 1997 to mid 2001), this amounts to a five-fold increase in news coverage.

Conventional wisdom – informed by a steady stream of political rhetoric – says that this is a response to the increasing risk posed by global terrorism since the attack on the twin towers. Indeed, the British government's recent leaflet advising citizens what to do in the event of an attack – together with a succession of warnings from the US government – imply the risk has reached unprecedented levels. And yet what is strikingly absent from both public discussion or news coverage is that there is little concrete evidence to support this view.

The US government's own figures on international terrorism – which it defines as the targeting of non-combatants or property by non-state agents and includes the actions of groups like the IRA, the UDF and Eta – suggests that the most active period of international terrorist activity was the mid-80s. With occasional blips – such as 1991 and 1999 to 2001 – the annual number of terrorist attacks has been in general decline since then.

The evidence suggests that the attack on 9/11 was not the dawn of a new era of global terrorism, but a devastating one-off. Indeed, the years since then have seen fewer incidents per year than at any time in the last 20 years. The recent annual rate is only a third of the level reached between 1985 and 1988.

> *Since January 2002, the Times, Financial Times, the Guardian, the Mail and the Mirror, have, between them, run an average of 400 stories about international terrorism every year*

But surely the attacks in the US, Bali and Madrid show that the scale of terrorist attacks has escalated, even if there are fewer of them? Well, again, the figures tell a different story. In terms of the number of casualties of international terrorism from 1998 to 2003, the peak year was not 2001, as most people might assume. Despite the 4,465 casualties on 9/11 (which alone accounted for 77% of casualties that year) there were more victims from international terrorist attacks three years earlier, in 1998.

The fact that 80% of the casualties that year were in Africa might partly explain (though by no means excuse) the lack of political and media interest. But this explanation only goes so far: after all, many of the 1998 incidents involved attacks by al-Qaida on US targets, and there were also a comparatively high number of casualties (405) that year in western Europe.

Indeed, a closer look at the last 20 years of media coverage of international terrorism reveals that there is little relation between the number of international terrorist incidents in any given year and the use of the term in the press.

If we take the *Times, Financial Times* and the *Guardian*, for example, we see fluctuations in media coverage that bear little relation to global trends. International terrorism

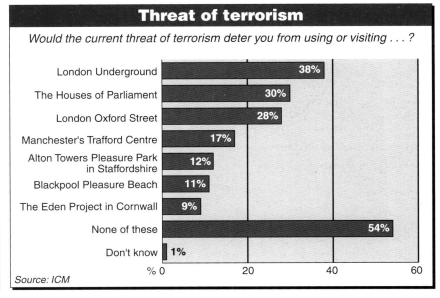

Threat of terrorism

Would the current threat of terrorism deter you from using or visiting . . . ?

London Underground	38%
The Houses of Parliament	30%
London Oxford Street	28%
Manchester's Trafford Centre	17%
Alton Towers Pleasure Park in Staffordshire	12%
Blackpool Pleasure Beach	11%
The Eden Project in Cornwall	9%
None of these	54%
Don't know	1%

Source: ICM

became highly newsworthy in 1986 (receiving more mentions than any of the last 20 years except 2001). This was the year in which Libya became the bête noire of international terrorism, and President Reagan ordered the bombing of Tripoli. But while the US data show an increase in the number of terrorist attacks in 1987, news coverage that year dropped significantly, to less than a quarter of the 1986 level.

But the biggest mismatch between the coverage of terrorism and terrorist incidents is, without doubt, the period from 2002 to the present day. News coverage is at its highest-ever sustained level, while there have been fewer terrorist attacks than at any time in the last two decades.

How to explain this discrepancy? Well, unfortunately, it's not unusual to see media coverage bear little relation to actual levels of risk. Media research on agenda-setting shows that – whether the topic is crime, drugs, war or the environment – there is often little relation between the volume of coverage and real-world trends.

In many instances, what the media are responding to is not an increase in the problem but an increase of political rhetoric. Both the war on drugs and the war on terror boosted media coverage which, in turn, justified a series of political initiatives.

This, combined with the US-centric nature of British news media, meant that the idea that 'the world changed' on 9/11 became a self-fulfilling prophecy. So, just as the war on drugs in the US in the late 80s led to a massive increase in news coverage about the issue – while drug use remained fairly static – so the war on terror has made every act, threat or worry about terrorism far more newsworthy than hitherto.

This kind of coverage distorts our perception of risk. So, despite the government's chief scientific adviser's warning that global warming is a much greater threat to life than global terrorism, terrorism ranks high on the public's list of concerns, while climate change scarcely registers. Worse, it creates a news climate – in the US at least – where politicians can expend considerable energy and public money on the war on terror while issues like global warming can be brushed aside.

■ Justin Lewis is professor of communication at the Cardiff School of Journalism, Media and Cultural Studies.

Ability to reason vital in fighting terrorism

Secretary-General Kofi Annan made the following remarks in September 2003 at a conference on 'Fighting Terrorism for Humanity: A Conference on the Roots of Evil'.

Terrorism has threatened Member States of the United Nations for many years, and the Organisation remains active against it on many fronts. Recently, the United Nations itself has been the target of a vicious and heartless terrorist attack, in which many irreplaceable colleagues and friends were killed. I am deeply saddened by their loss. They were some of our best.

If we are to fight terrorism effectively, and avoid mistakes in doing so, we need more debate, not less, regarding possible policy responses. I hope my short remarks this morning contain some ideas that can contribute to that debate.

Terrorism is a global threat, and it can never be justified. No end can give anyone the right to kill innocent civilians. On the contrary, the use of terrorism to pursue any cause – even a worthy one – can only defile that cause, and thereby damage it.

While terrorism is an evil with which there can be no compromise, we must use our heads, not our hearts, in deciding our response. The rage

we feel at terrorist attacks must not remove our ability to reason. If we are to defeat terrorism, it is our duty, and indeed our interest, to try to understand this deadly phenomenon, and carefully to examine what works, and what does not, in fighting it.

The experts who met in Oslo in June to contribute ideas to today's discussion rightly pointed out that terrorists are often rational and intentional actors who develop deliberate strategies to achieve political objectives. We should not pretend that all terrorists are simply insane, or that the decision to resort to terrorism is unrelated to the political, social and economic situation in which people find themselves. But we are also mistaken if we assume, equally, that terrorists are mere products of their environment. The phenomenon is more complex than that.

We also delude ourselves if we think that military force alone can defeat terrorism. It may sometimes be necessary to use force to counter terrorist groups. But we need to do much more than that if terrorism is to be stopped.

Terrorists thrive on despair. They may gain recruits or supporters where peaceful and legitimate ways of redressing a grievance do not exist, or appear to have been exhausted. By this process, power is taken away from people and placed in the hands of small and shadowy groups.

But the fact that a few wicked men or women commit murder in its name does not make a cause any less just. Nor does it relieve us of the obligation to deal with legitimate grievance. On the contrary, terrorism will only be defeated if we act to solve the political disputes and long-standing conflicts which generate support for it. If we do not, we shall find ourselves acting as a recruiting sergeant for the very terrorists we seek to suppress.

We should also remember that, in the fight against terrorism, ideas matter. We must articulate a powerful and compelling global vision that can defeat the vivid, if extreme, visions of some terrorist groups. We must make clear, by word and deed, not only that we are fighting terrorists, but also that we are standing, indeed fighting, for something – for peace, for resolution of conflict, for human rights and development.

Accordingly, there needs to be more on the horizon than simply winning a war against terrorism. There must be the promise of a better and fairer world, and a concrete plan to get there. For this reason, the vision of the Millennium Declaration has become more, not less, important, as has the need to take action to turn its promise into reality.

We must never, in the fight against terrorism, lower our standards to theirs. States therefore need to ensure that, in fighting terrorists, they respect the limits which international humanitarian law places on the use of force. The failure to do so can erode our shared values.

We should also remember that, in the fight against terrorism, ideas matter. We must articulate a powerful and compelling global vision that can defeat the vivid, if extreme, visions of some terrorist groups

---

Paradoxically, terrorist groups may actually be sustained when, in responding to their outrages, governments cross the line and commit outrages themselves – whether it is ethnic cleansing, the indiscriminate bombardment of cities, the torture of prisoners, targeted assassinations, or accepting the death of innocent civilians as 'collateral damage'. These acts are not only illegal and unjustifiable. They may also be exploited by terrorists to gain new followers, and to generate cycles of violence in which they thrive.

For these reasons, and for many others, I believe that there is no trade-off to be made between human rights and terrorism. Upholding human rights is not at odds with battling terrorism: on the contrary, the moral vision of human rights – the deep respect for the dignity of each person – is among our most powerful weapons against it.

To compromise on the protection of human rights would hand terrorists a victory they cannot achieve on their own. The promotion and protection of human rights, as well as the strict observance of international humanitarian law, should, therefore, be at the centre of anti-terrorism strategies.

To fight terrorism, we must not only fight terrorists. We have to win hearts and minds. To do this, we should act to resolve political disputes, articulate and work towards a vision of peace and development, and promote human rights. And we can only do all this effectively if we work together, through multilateral institutions – first and foremost, through the United Nations.

If these ideas guide us in shaping our response to terrorism, our moral position in the fight against terrorism will be assured. And we will not hand terrorists a victory, but a stinging rejection, both of their methods and their world view.

■ The above information is from the United Nation Press Release SG/SM/8885. For further information visit their website: www.un.org

© United Nations

What does Islam say about terrorism?

Islam, a religion of mercy, does not permit terrorism. In the Quran, God has said: 'God does not forbid you from showing kindness and dealing justly with those who have not fought you about religion and have not driven you out of your homes. God loves just dealers.' (Quran, 60:8)

The Prophet Muhammad used to prohibit soldiers from killing women and children,[1] and he would advise them: . . . Do not betray, do not be excessive, do not kill a newborn child.[2] And he also said: Whoever has killed a person having a treaty with the Muslims shall not smell the fragrance of Paradise, though its fragrance is found for a span of forty years.[3]

Also, the Prophet Muhammad has forbidden punishment with fire.[4]

He once listed murder as the second of the major sins,[5] and he even warned that on the Day of Judgment, The first cases to be adjudicated between people on the Day of Judgment will be those of bloodshed.[6,7]

Muslims are even encouraged to be kind to animals and are forbidden to hurt them. Once the Prophet Muhammad said: A woman was punished because she imprisoned a cat until it died. On account of this, she was doomed to Hell. While she imprisoned it, she did not give the cat food or drink, nor did she free it to eat the insects of the earth.[8]

He also said that a man gave a very thirsty dog a drink, so God forgave his sins for this action. The Prophet was asked, 'Messenger of God, are we rewarded for kindness towards animals?' He said: There is a reward for kindness to every living animal or human.[9]

Additionally, while taking the life of an animal for food, Muslims are commanded to do so in a manner that causes the least amount of fright and suffering possible. The Prophet Muhammad said: When you slaughter an animal, do so in the best way. One should sharpen his knife to reduce the suffering of the animal.[10]

In light of these and other Islamic texts, the act of inciting terror in the hearts of defenceless civilians, the wholesale destruction of buildings and properties, the bombing and maiming of innocent men, women, and children are all forbidden and detestable acts according to Islam and the Muslims. Muslims follow a religion of peace, mercy, and forgiveness, and the vast majority have nothing to do with the violent events some have associated with Muslims. If an individual Muslim were to commit an act of terrorism, this person would be guilty of violating the laws of Islam.

If an individual Muslim were to commit an act of terrorism, this person would be guilty of violating the laws of Islam

Footnotes:

1 Narrated in *Saheeh Muslim*, #1744, and *Saheeh Al-Bukhari*, #3015.
2 Narrated in *Saheeh Muslim*, #1731, and *Al-Tirmizi*, #1408.
3 Narrated in *Saheeh Al-Bukhari*, #3166, and *Ibn Majah*, #2686.
4 Narrated in *Abu-Dawood*, #2675.
5 Narrated in *Saheeh Al-Bukhari*, #6871, and *Saheeh Muslim*, #88.
6 This means killing and injuring.
7 Narrated in *Saheeh Muslim*, #1678, and *Saheeh Al-Bukhari*, #6533.
8 Narrated in *Saheeh Muslim*, #2422, and *Saheeh Al-Bukhari*, #2365.
9 This saying of Muhammad has been mentioned in more detail on this page. Narrated in *Saheeh Muslim*, #2244, and *Saheeh Al-Bukhari*, #2466.
10 Narrated in *Saheeh Muslim*, #1955, and *Al-Tirmizi*, #1409.

■ The above information is from *A Brief Illustrated Guide To Understanding Islam*'s website which can be found at www.islam-guide.com

© *www.islam-guide.com*

Who are the terrorists?

Information from the Institute of Race Relations

Discussion of the UK's tough anti-terrorist laws has focused on the low conviction rate for those arrested under their powers. What is ignored is that, of those who are convicted, many are not Muslim but are White Loyalists and/or racists.

According to Home Office figures, since 11 September 2001, 609 people have been arrested and 99 of them have been charged with offences under the Terrorism Act 2000. And, as of 30 June 2004, there had been fifteen convictions.

It is easy to assume that all of these convictions were of Muslims, given the recent high-profile arrests and the media coverage of them. For example, after the arrest of thirteen men on 3 August 2004, the *Sunday Express* headline of 8 August 2004 read, 'Cyanide terror of cola bombs'. The *News of the World*'s read, '9/11 on the tube'.

Cases dropped

The Institute of Race Relations has documented eleven of these fifteen convictions. According to the research, only three Muslims have actually been convicted under the 2000 Act and two of those have been given leave to appeal their convictions. Furthermore, at least twenty-one Muslims, whose charges were actually brought to court, have had the cases against them dropped or they were not proven. Countless others have been arrested in high-profile raids under anti-terrorism laws, charged with 'terrorist' offences and then quietly released without charge, or re-arrested by the immigration service or charged with other criminal offences.

But six of those convicted under the Terrorism Act 2000 are White and were convicted for offences such as wearing a ring or carrying a flag

INSTITUTE OF RACE RELATIONS

with the symbols of banned Loyalist organisations. The 2000 Act makes it illegal even to wear a T-shirt supporting a banned organisation. A further two non-Muslims have been convicted under the Anti-Terrorism, Crime and Security Act 2001.

White convictions under the Terrorism Act 2000

Six White men have been convicted under the Terrorism Act 2000. They were all found to be involved in proscribed Loyalist groups: the Loyalist Volunteer Force, Ulster Freedom Fighters (UFF) and the Ulster Volunteer Force (UVF). The convicted men include Alan Robert Ferguson, Stephen Walker, Robert Warnock and Jamie Clarke – all of whom were jailed for displaying

Loyalist paramilitary flags of the Loyalist Volunteer Force in the Loughview estate in Holywood, Co. Down.

James Rankin was convicted for wearing a ring bearing the symbols of the UVF, which was 'likely to arouse suspicion' that he was a member or supporter of the group. The 42-year-old Scottish man appealed against his conviction in June 2004 and lost. Another man, 19-year-old Grant O'Donnell, was convicted of being a member of the UFF but he has successfully appealed against the conviction.

White convictions under the Anti-Terrorism, Crime and Security Act 2001

Another two White people have been convicted under the Anti-Terrorism, Crime and Security Act 2001 (ATCSA), one for a racist hate mail campaign. Ian MacIntosh and 17-year-old schoolboy Paul Smith both pleaded guilty in separate cases to charges of sending letters containing 'substances claiming to be noxious'.

■ In October 2003, Ian MacIntosh pleaded guilty to a charge under

the ATCSA and was sentenced to 150 hours' community service after psychiatrists said he was suffering from a mental illness at the time of the offences. He admitted sending a letter to the office of Mohammad Sarwar MP containing white powder, 'with the intention of inducing in the MP or a member of his staff a belief that it contained a noxious substance that would endanger life or create a serious heath risk'. The letter also contained racist threats. He also pleaded guilty to sending racist hate mail to four others between May 1999 and May 2003.

- Paul Smith was sentenced to three years in a young offenders' institute and a 12-month supervision order. He pleaded guilty to charges under the ATCSA – preparing and transmitting letters whereby the powder inside was deposited and inhaled by people opening them, all to their fear and alarm. He sent threatening letters with powdered 'poison' between 20 August 2001 and 7 February 2002 to prominent people. Smith, who was aged 15 when the offences took place, was recruited by an unnamed Scottish Republican group. He never met the older man who 'groomed him' on the internet but agreed to send letters to 44 people containing powder with claimed to be ricin or anthrax – in fact, it was harmless.

Convicted for wearing a shirt

Since 30 June 2004, another White man has been convicted of an offence under the Terrorism Act 2000. Earlier this month, 32-year-old Alexander Hood pleaded guilty to wearing a shirt bearing the logo of a banned organisation – the Ulster Volunteer Force. He was fined £250. He was arrested after going to the High Court in Kilmarnock where friends were on trial for arms and explosives offences.

A full report on arrests and convictions under the anti-terror laws will be published shortly. The Institute of Race Relations is monitoring arrests under anti-terror laws and how they affect minority ethnic communities and especially asylum seekers in the UK. If you have been arrested, or know anyone who has, and want to tell us (in confidence) about your experiences, please email info@irr.org.uk with details.

The Institute of Race Relations is precluded from expressing a corporate view: any opinions expressed are therefore those of the authors.

- The above information is from the Institute of Race Relation's website which can be found at www.irr.org.uk

'We must unite to defeat this threat'

The Muslim Council of Britain took the exceptional step of writing to the Imams and Chairmen of each and every mosque in the UK – over 1000 of them – calling upon them to observe the utmost vigilance in the face of a common terror threat that hangs over us all (2 April 2004).

The MCB letter has been issued in the wake of March 2004 atrocious bombings of the Madrid trains. There can be little doubt now that our country has become a premium target for terrorists.

The huge counter-terrorist operation in March 2004 involving over 700 Police officers across London and the Home Counties which saw twenty-four premises searched, eight men of Pakistani descent arrested together with the seizure of half a ton of ammonium nitrate will inevitably be seen as

By Inayat Bunglawala, Secretary, The Muslim Council of Britain

evidence of the increased threat facing our country from terrorists.

At the Muslim Council of Britain, we see it as the duty of all Britons, Muslims and non-Muslims, to work together to thwart any danger to this country and its inhabitants.

Yet, very often, British Muslims have been told that they have not condemned terrorists loudly enough and need to do more. The semi-literate lecture in Italy in March 2004 by Lord Carey admonishing Muslims for being backward and not speaking out against suicide bombers was a classic case in point.

This time though, it was heartening to see Peter Clarke, Head of the Metropolitan Police's Anti-Terrorist branch, making it clear that: 'the overwhelming majority of the Muslim community are law abiding and completely reject all forms of violence'.

Clarke even urged the media to refrain from using the term 'Islamic terrorist' – a term which has caused a lot of hurt to British Muslims because of the utter incompatibility of the teachings of Islam and the blessed Prophet Muhammad with the vile and destructive phenomenon of terrorism.

Still, the immediate spotlight will fall on Britain's two-million-strong Muslim community. The British press has been awash with provocative stories since 9/11 about the inflammatory rantings of Abu Hamza and Omar Bakri. Yet the wild level of coverage given to these two loudmouths is out of all proportion to their minuscule following in this country and has arguably helped them to further their divisive agenda to the detriment of good relations between Muslims and non-Muslims.

This is not to ignore the real possibility that there may well be a tiny group of Muslims who have decided to embark upon the path of violence. They should be caught and tried according to the law. If found guilty, then the full weight of the judicial system ought to be brought to bear on them. We will have no sympathy for those who plan to endanger the lives of innocent people.

The Qur'an teaches us:

'He who killed any person, unless it be a person guilty of manslaughter, or of spreading chaos in the land, should be looked upon as though he had slain all mankind, and he who saved one life should be regarded as though he had saved the lives of all mankind.' (al-Qur'an 5:32)

We in the Muslim community need to do everything we can to ensure that mischievous or criminal elements are prevented from infiltrating our community and provoking any unlawful activity. Certainly, any suspected criminal activity should be reported to the police.

Our youth should be provided with correct Islamic guidance and not left to be preyed upon by ideologues with sinister motives.

Muslim communities around the country need to liaise with the local police and give them the fullest cooperation in dealing with any criminal activity including possible terrorist threats.

'Help one another to virtue and God-consciousness and do not help one other to sin and transgression.' (al-Qur'an 5:2)

Once in receipt of this information, it is then the duty of the police to verify the exact nature of the threat.

A real concern we do have is that these arrests should be seen in the wider context of events in this country since 9/11. Many of you will recall reading about the arrests in November 2002 of six men for allegedly plotting a cyanide gas attack on the London Underground. Do you, however, remember reading anything further about that case, such as a trial hearing or any convictions being secured for that dastardly plot? No, neither can I.

Similarly, you will recall the high-profile police raid on the Finsbury Park mosque in January 2003 involving some 150 police officers. Seven men were arrested at that time. All, except for one man – who was charged with immigration offences – were later released.

We in the Muslim community need to do everything we can to ensure that mischievous or criminal elements are prevented from infiltrating our community and provoking any unlawful activity

---

There are a number of other examples of incidents that have received prominent media attention only for the individuals to be subsequently released without any charges brought against them. The impact of such ordeals on the persons concerned and their families is usually crushing.

Indeed, according to Home Office figures, between 9/11 and 31st December 2003, 537 people were arrested under anti-terror legislation, with 94 of them being charged with terrorist-related offences; 263 people were released without charge and only 6 convictions had actually been secured.

The British Muslim community has faced a severe backlash following the Madrid bombings. Just last week, in Plumstead, south-east London, over 40 graves were desecrated in a Muslim cemetery. In Ilford in April 2004, a Christian fanatic abducted a Muslim schoolgirl and with a razor blade slashed crosses on her hand, upper arms and side, while demanding that she recite the Trinity during an hour-long ordeal.

So we would urge caution from all concerned in the wake of this worrying development.

We have been told in recent weeks by the Prime Minister Tony Blair, the Home Secretary David Blunkett and the Metropolitan Police Commissioner Sir John Stevens that our country is facing an unprecedented terror threat. Who can now doubt them?

All of us, Muslims and non-Muslims, need to work in a united manner to defeat it.

■ This article first appeared in the *Daily Express*.
© The Muslim Council of Britain

Home Office draws up tighter terrorism laws

By Alan Travis, Home Affairs Editor

David Blunkett, the home secretary, is believed to be close to backing a specific criminal offence of 'acts preparatory to terrorism' as part of his extension of anti-terror legislation planned for this autumn.

This has been repeatedly urged by the Liberal Democrat peer, Lord Carlile, who has carried out the official reviews of the emergency anti-terror legislation. He argues that such a law would allow suspected international terrorists being interned indefinitely in Britain to face criminal trials instead.

Mr Blunkett is expected to introduce the new 'broadly drawn' offence of acts preparatory to terrorism alongside the renewal of his emergency powers to detain foreign nationals who are certified as suspected international terrorists – known as executive detention powers.

He is also considering introducing new civil orders to restrict the activities of people linked to terrorism but who are not themselves considered serious terrorist suspects.

The overhaul of the anti-terror laws is being considered as American banks in London step up security after the discovery of detailed but dated plans for al-Qaida attacks in the US and Britain.

The Home Office said no specific threat had emerged about Britain, adding: 'We are maintaining a state of heightened readiness in the UK.'

The new counter-terror package is expected to spark sharp criticism from civil liberties groups, who will be dismayed that Mr Blunkett has not used the opportunity to replace his emergency executive detention powers with realistic alternatives.

New legislation is needed to renew the powers or they will lapse in November 2006 under the 'sunset clause' in the original emergency legislation passed in the immediate aftermath of the September 11 attacks.

The official consultation on the government's new counter-terrorism package will close at the end of the August 2004 with final decisions expected before November 2004.

It is expected that the emergency powers will continue to be used only against those who are suspected of being members of the al-Qaida network and their immediate associates.

> *The overhaul of the anti-terror laws is being considered as American banks in London step up security after the discovery of detailed but dated plans for al-Qaida attacks in the US and Britain*

The package will amalgamate the Terrorism Act 2000, which deals with domestic terrorism, and the Anti-Terrorism, Crime and Security Act 2001, which deals with suspected international terrorists.

The home secretary has already been forced to drop his ideas of reducing the standard of proof in terrorist cases and holding pre-emptive trials with secret evidence heard before vetted counsel in the face of open opposition from the attorney general and the director of public prosecutions, among others.

It is believed that the security services also continue to oppose his more widely-supported plans to lift the ban on telephone tap evidence being used in British criminal trials in an attempt to secure more prosecutions as an alternative to executive detention without trial.

The Home Office is working on producing a way of using intercept evidence in court without contravening the European Convention on Human Rights and with safeguards to prevent the disclosure of 'sensitive capabilities' – information revealing how the security services go about their business.

Mr Blunkett is also expected to announce this year that new powers to extend the scale of US-style 'plea bargaining' in cases involving organised crime and drug smuggling will now cover terrorist cases.

The review of the anti-terrorism laws, which are to form a major plank of the government's legislative programme this autumn, is likely to suffer a fresh setback when a cross-party group of MPs and peers is expected to publish a highly critical report.

The report from the joint parliamentary committee on human rights is likely to give its strong backing to alternatives to the renewal of the emergency powers of detention without trial of suspected international terrorists.

The 'internment' powers involve the British government in a continued 'opt-out' from the European Convention on Human Rights.

Terrorism

Frequently asked questions

What should I do if there is a terrorist attack?

If you are at the site of an incident, follow the instructions of the emergency services.

If it is a major incident, and you are not in the immediate area, our advice is to 'go in, stay in, tune in'. Go home or go inside some other safe location, stay indoors and tune in to local radio or television news programmes for advice and information. We will issue advice immediately if you need to take specific action.

It is always sensible to have a battery-powered or wind-up radio in the house to prepare for a range of emergencies, including power cuts and floods. For further information see the commonsense advice on the Planning for Emergencies Website.

How will I know what to do if there is a chemical or biological incident? And why can't you tell us more in advance?

There is no such thing as a standard chemical or biological incident, and therefore no such thing as a standard response.

Our response to a chemical or biological incident – accidental or otherwise – would depend on a number of factors. The emergency services are best placed to decide the appropriate response, taking into account the relevant factors.

To give detailed advice in advance about how to handle every potential threat would be misleading and unhelpful. Worse, it could lead to confusion in an actual incident – the advice given for one type of situation might be wrong in different circumstances.

We, and the emergency services, will provide immediate information and advice in the event of a discernible threat or a specific incident.

At the moment, we do not believe that the best way to offer useful, up-to-date advice is to issue a national leaflet.

Do I need to buy a gas mask or protective suit to protect myself from chemical or biological threats? And do I need to stockpile food, water, or anything else?

No. There is currently no information that would lead us to advise you to obtain protective clothing, including gas masks, or to take other special precautions.

However, it is always sensible to be prepared for a range of emergencies, including severe weather or floods.

We will issue advice immediately if you need to take specific action.

There has been a lot of media coverage about people getting smallpox vaccinations. Do I need a vaccination and can I get one from my GP?

No. Smallpox was declared eradicated in 1980. Consequently, smallpox vaccinations are not available on the NHS through family doctors and General Practitioners do not hold stocks of the vaccine.

It is always sensible to have a battery-powered or wind-up radio in the house to prepare for a range of emergencies, including power cuts

---

The Department of Health holds a strategic stock for use in an emergency, which can and will be distributed quickly in the event of a bio-terrorism incident involving smallpox, but they are not currently recommending vaccination for the wider UK public. This decision follows World Health Organisation guidelines about how best to protect the public. It has not been taken lightly, and the situation is being kept under very careful review.

The Department of Health have recommended vaccination for a small number of frontline health-service staff and military personnel. This is because these frontline staff and personnel would provide the first response if there were a confirmed, suspected or threatened release of smallpox.

Contingency plans for dealing with smallpox are detailed in the draft guidelines on smallpox available at http://www.doh.gov.uk/epcu/cbr/biol/smallpoxplan.htm

Is it safe to visit and travel around London?

London has lived with the threat of terrorism for more than 30 years. Operational responses are well co-ordinated, regularly practised and continually reviewed.

Since September 11 2001, additional measures have been taken, including specific counter-terrorism funding to the Metropolitan Police and detailed work by London Underground with the emergency services and security services to ensure systems are in place to deter or deal with an attack.

Strategic emergency planning for the Capital is lead by the London Resilience Forum (LRF). The LRF considers all aspects of the threat against the Capital and has contingency plans in place, which are regularly exercised.

The LRF is chaired by Nick Raynsford as Minister for London Resilience, with the Mayor as his deputy, and comprises the heads of the emergency services and London Underground, plus senior-level representatives from the city's local authorities and utilities, as well as the Home Office and the Cabinet Office.

More information is available at www.londonprepared.gov.uk

Is there anyone I should be looking out for specifically?

It is their actions that give terrorists away, not their appearances. While you should stay alert to suspicious behaviour, it is very important to remember that terrorism affects us all. No community or religion should be made a scapegoat for the actions of terrorists. People of many faiths died on September 11, and the leaders of all faiths condemned the attacks.

We have a clear vision of a multi-cultural Britain – one that values the contribution made by each of our many ethnic, cultural and faith communities.

We are determined to see a truly dynamic society, in which people from different backgrounds can live and work together – whilst retaining their distinctive identities – in an atmosphere of mutual respect and understanding.

If you see harassment or discrimination, do not ignore it. It is everyone's responsibility to prevent it.

What if there is a terrorist attack and my children are at school?

In the event of a specific terrorist threat or incident, the local police will work with schools to ensure they are protected and to enact their

---

If you see harassment or discrimination, do not ignore it. It is everyone's responsibility to prevent it

---

emergency plans as necessary. The action taken would depend on the incident itself, and would not be different from the emergency plans that schools already have for fire evacuations and bomb threats.

All schools and Local Education Authorities in England have been made aware that they can access guidance on dealing with terrorism via the UK Resilience website at http://www.ukresilience.info Many local authorities have also issued guidance to schools in their area to assist in emergency planning.

Is it safe to fly?

- The UK aviation security regime is one of the most developed in the world. It was further tightened in the aftermath of the September 11 attacks in the United States. The programme is kept under permanent review and adjusted when necessary.
- Our aviation security programme works on many levels, with measures for all stages of the process – from check-in through to the flight itself. Not all of the measures are obvious: a lot goes on behind the scenes.
- In May 2002 the Home Office and the Department for Transport appointed Sir John Wheeler to carry out a major independent review of airport security and policing. With the Department for Transport, we accepted and are now implementing the additional measures recom-

mended in his October 2002 report.

- Security measures on the ground currently include an enhanced passenger searching regime, and a tightening up of the articles that cannot be taken into an aircraft cabin.
- Amongst in-flight security measures are regulations ensuring that cockpit doors on all aircraft leaving the UK and using UK airspace are locked. We are also implementing a requirement to fit strengthened cockpit doors, six months ahead of the international deadline.
- In 2002, we also decided to reinforce the existing package of measures for in-flight security by developing a capability to place covert, specially trained armed police officers aboard UK civil aircraft, should that be warranted.
- For more information, go to http://www.aviation.dft.gov.uk/index.htm

What about my pets or animals?

The handling of animals, including pets, would depend very much on the particular circumstances of an incident. In drawing up contingency plans following the deliberate release of biological agents, such as infectious diseases, we have given consideration to the handling of animals.

If you can't find the information you need, take a look at our Press Releases & Publications section. There you'll find up-to-date press releases, reports and documents about the terrorist threat and what's being done to combat it in the UK.

Alternatively, find out what you can do to protect yourself against terrorism in your everyday life: at home, at work and when you're travelling.

Finally, if you can provide any information about terrorism, or feel that you're in any immediate danger, there are a number of ways to contact us. For full contact details visit our website at www.homeoffice.gov.uk

- The above information is from the Home Office's website which can be found at www.homeoffice.gov.uk
  © Crown copyright

Counter-terrorism and resilience: key facts

Since September 11 2001, the Government has substantially increased the country's counter-terrorism efforts and has improved contingency planning and resilience to a range of emergencies.

The Government has set itself the strategic goal of 'reducing the risk from international terrorism so that our people can go about their business freely and with confidence'.

Reducing the risks breaks down into four broad mission areas:

- Preventing terrorism by tackling its underlying causes;
- Pursuing terrorists and those that sponsor them;
- Protecting the public and UK interests; and
- Preparing for the consequences.
All underpinned by intelligence and public communication.

The Government has:

- Toughened already tough counter-terrorism legislation, and worked to establish a new legislative framework for civil protection
- Provided significant new resources for counter-terrorism and to strengthen national resilience, with resources for national security measures doubling by 2008. This includes:
- £85.5m to the NHS to counter bioterrorism;
- £56m to the fire service for mass decontamination programmes plus up to £132m funding on search and rescue;
- £49m to the Metropolitan Police for counter-terrorism work;
- a doubling of resources for local authority emergency planning;
- £12m to police forces outside London;
- £15m to help Special Branches in police forces which will significantly increase their surveillance and intelligence gathering capabilities to prevent attacks against the UK; and
- additional funding for the

Security Service to boost capacity to collect, analyse and act on information and intelligence. Over the next few years the number of staff will increase by 50%.

- Strengthened immigration provisions to ensure that those who present a security risk cannot hide behind refugee protections
- Tightened port, airport and border security
- Proscribed new terrorist organisations
- Streamlined and speeded up extradition procedures
- Frozen the assets of international terrorist organisations
- Given police more powers to help the fight against international terrorism
- Increased joint working and intelligence-sharing between governments and law enforcement agencies across the world
- Worked with the police to strengthen links to protect and reassure minority faith communities
- Continued its programme of major exercises specifically dealing with terrorist scenarios
- Tightened controls on dangerous materials
- Established a cross-Government Chemical, Biological, Radiological and Nuclear (CBRN) Resilience Programme, which aims to:
- improve co-ordination of CBRN research across Government;
- focus CBRN research on develop-

ing the capabilities needed for a resilient response;

- be linked to anticipated developments in the threat so that enhanced capability is available at the correct time;
- provide the evidence base upon which to build policy and planning decisions; and
- fill capability gaps and ensure resources are allocated to the highest priority programmes.
- Put in place a well-developed structure for emergency planning across the country with police, fire and ambulance services working together
- Put in place regional resilience structures in the nine English regions with similar arrangements in the devolved administrations
- Continued to improve levels of equipment for the emergency services, including 80 purpose-built vehicles for the Fire Service in England and Wales and a range of search and rescue equipment, such as radiation detectors, specialist search cameras and almost 5,000 new gas-tight suits.

Legislation

The Government has toughened already tough anti-terror laws. The key pieces of legislation are:

Terrorism Act 2000

The Terrorism Act is the primary piece of UK counter-terrorist legislation and it has proved a vital tool in the fight against terrorism. Key measures include:

- outlawing certain terrorist groups and making it illegal for them to operate in the UK
- giving police enhanced powers to investigate terrorism
- creating new criminal offences, including:
- inciting terrorist acts,
- seeking or providing training for terrorist purposes at home or overseas,

- providing instruction or training in the use of firearms, explosives or chemical, biological or nuclear weapons.

Anti-Terrorism, Crime and Security Act 2001 (ATCSA)

The Anti-Terrorism, Crime and Security Act was passed in the immediate aftermath of the September 11 attacks. Key measures include:

- preventing terrorists from abusing immigration procedures by allowing the Home Secretary to detain foreign nationals who are suspected of involvement in international terrorism but who cannot immediately be removed from the UK, until we can deport them;
- strengthening the protection and security of aviation and civil nuclear sites, and tightening the security of dangerous substances held in labs and universities;
- cutting off terrorists from their funds by allowing assets to be frozen at the start of an investigation.

Civil Contingencies Bill

Currently going through Parliament, this Bill will deliver a single framework for civil protection to meet the challenges of the 21st century.

Public information

Ever since 9/11, the Government has made it a priority to be open and honest with the public about the level and nature of the threat we face. Through new websites, publications, speeches and Parliamentary updates, Ministers have ensured that the amount of information on security matters that is publicly available has increased.

This must be done in a way that does not compromise security or unnecessarily raise fears. It is important that the public knows what basic self-protection steps to take, and understands the work going on behind the scenes to protect us all.

Government departments and the police continue to work together to develop further public information

to help people maintain vigilance and prepare for the consequences of serious incidents.

A public information booklet, *Preparing for Emergencies – what you need to know*, has been delivered to 25 million households in the UK. It contains practical advice on how to prepare for a range of emergencies.

Further information for the general public, emergency planners or businesses can be found on the following websites:
www.preparingforemergencies.gov.uk
www.homeoffice.gov.uk/terrorism
www.ukresilience.info
www.mi5.gov.uk
www.londonprepared.gov.uk

© Crown Copyright

MI5 website lists 10 anti-terrorist tips

By Philip Johnston, Home Affairs Editor

MI5 has published security advice for businesses and other organisations worried that they could be terrorist targets. It described the threat 30 April 2004 as 'real and serious' on a new website.

A list of 10 safety tips include carrying out risk assessments, examining mail-handling procedures, checking that staff are who they say they are and protecting workers against flying glass by applying transparent anti-shatter film to windows.

MI5 urges companies to develop 'security awareness', train staff in emergency procedures and ensure that responsibility for security is invested in someone at board level.

The security service has been providing advice to business on a confidential basis for years, but Eliza Manningham-Buller, the director general, said it should be made more widely available.

Despite the preoccupation with the threat from international terrorism, figures issued by Washington suggest that the number of attacks is lower than at any time for 30 years.

The State Department's annual report said yesterday that deaths caused by terrorism last year were half the number of 2002. There has been no international terrorist attack on British soil since a bomb exploded outside the Israeli embassy in London in 1994, although several attempts have been thwarted.

Nevertheless, MI5 said the danger to Britain and its interests overseas from al-Qa'eda and associated groups had 'grown substantially' in recent years. Extra vigilance was needed.

'Osama bin Laden has in several statements publicly named Britain and British interests as a target and encouraged attacks to be carried out against them,' the service said.

'The events in Madrid demonstrated the capability of an al-Qa'eda affiliated terrorist group to carry out an attack without warning against a civilian target in western Europe.'

David Blunkett, the Home Secretary, said: 'The risk from terrorism is very real and we have a duty to ensure that individuals and businesses are armed with the information that allows them to take sensible and proportionate steps to protect themselves from new and emerging threats.'

James Hart, the deputy commissioner of the City of London Police, said the website would be 'an enormous advantage' to the counter-terrorism effort.

He repeated the recent statement of Sir John Stevens, the Metropolitan Police commissioner, that a terrorist attack on Britain was 'inevitable'.

© *Telegraph Group Limited, London 2004*

Internment in Britain

Information from Liberty

Direct access to full legal representation. A full understanding of the charges levelled against you. A hearing in a court. And in front of a jury. These are crucial to any sense of justice. Alas, not in Britain 2004.

Under the Anti-Terrorism, Crime and Security Act of 2001, passed in the wake of the 9/11 atrocities, foreign nationals can be held in high security British prisons merely on the basis of the suspicion of a politician.

If the Home Secretary, David Blunkett, deems that you are a foreign national who cannot be deported and that you may have 'links' with a terrorist organisation, then you can expect these key principles to be ignored.

Over a dozen men remain interned in Belmarsh prison. Others are held in different jails up and down the country – some for more than two years. They do not know when they might be released or when they might see their families again. Their chances of a full and fair hearing in front of twelve jurors are minimal.

Camp Delta, the notorious detention facility in Guantanamo Bay, has attracted considerable publicity. At the time of going to press, nine British citizens remain imprisoned in this legal 'twilight zone'. The *Daily Mail* – not usually associated with civil liberties crusades – has been at the forefront of demanding their release. But in the shape of Belmarsh prison, the United Kingdom has its very own Camp Echo. An overlooked, almost forgotten, but chilling moral mirror of the law-free zone in Guantanamo Bay.

To enable detention without trial, the British government has had to opt out or 'derogate' from the European Convention of Human Rights. We are the only one of the dozens of signatories to have felt the need to do this. In justification, the formal public position of the Government is that the United Kingdom is presently in a state of emergency so great that the nation's very existence is threatened. Absolutely no undertakings have been given as to when, how or on what basis this extraordinary and bizarre analysis might be reconsidered.

Already, key opinion formers have begun to speak out. The Archbishop of Canterbury voiced his opposition in his Christmas message. A wide range of religious and community groups have also expressed their concerns. Liberty is pioneering the campaign to demand the immediate release or charge of the detainees. Working closely alongside their solicitors, we are determined to ensure that the so-called 'war on terror' is not a veil behind which British justice is dismantled.

Shami Chakrabarti, Liberty's Director, said: 'It is difficult to imagine anything which could concern British human rights activists more. Indefinite imprisonment on the basis of the hunch of a politician – however well meaning – is simply unacceptable in a civilised and democratic society. Once again, we have seen ill-thought-out "exceptional laws" passed in haste, acquiring a sinister potential permanence. It's time to call a halt.'

You can help this campaign by signing the petition on Liberty's website – www.liberty-human-rights.org.uk – and by writing to your Member of Parliament. In uncertain and insecure times, the defence of fundamental rights and liberties is a difficult but vital argument to advance. Liberty exists for precisely such a purpose and will not shrink from the challenge.

■ The above information is from Liberty's newsletter *Liberty*, Winter 2004. For further information, visit their website at www.liberty-human-rights.org.uk

© *Liberty*

Countering terrorism

Here are some things people have suggested should be done to counter the risks of terrorism. Others oppose them as they say they would endanger the rights of everyone. Bearing these two things in mind, for each one please say whether you would support or oppose the measure to counter terrorism

	Support	Oppose	Don't know
Indefinite detention of foreign terrorist suspects	62%	32%	6%
Indefinite detention of British terrorist suspects	63%	29%	8%
Indefinite detention of those associating with terror suspects	58%	34%	8%
All police to be routinely armed	47%	48%	5%
Bring in the death penalty for terrorist offences that kill people	59%	37%	4%
Give police greater powers to eavesdrop on people (like listening to telephone conversations and reading emails)	46%	50%	4%
Allow the use of phone tapping and other eavesdropping as evidence in court cases	63%	33%	4%
Police powers to stop and search anyone at any time	69%	29%	2%
Detain all immigrants and asylum seekers until they can be assessed as potential terror threats	66%	45%	6%
Make it easier to get conviction in cases involving terrorism by changing the rules in court so that someone can be convicted on the balance of probabilities rather than beyond all reasonable doubt	49%	45%	6%

ICM Research interviewed a random sample of 510 adults aged 18+ by telephone on 23-24 April 2004. Interviews were conducted across the country and the results have been weighted to the profile of all adults.

Source: ICM

Islamophobia – what is it?

Islamophobia is the prejudice against or hatred of Muslims. Some people are prejudiced against others because they're scared of people who are different, often because they're worried they will change their way of life and the areas where they live

Since the attacks on September 11th, and the following war on terrorism, young people have been able to read and watch loads more in the news about how the West sees Muslims. Protests outsides Mosques in London and other racial abuse towards Muslims, made us worry that Muslims are not safe in Britain. So, a group of reporters from Children's Express, a programme of learning through journalism, went out in North London to ask young people in the street what they think.

We found that most young people were not sure what they thought about the questions we asked. We think that people need to learn more about others, and then they won't be so worried.

George, 12

Have the attacks on September 11th changed how people feel about Muslims?
'I suppose, cause they blame all of them, even though it was a group of people.'

Is there a link between Islam and terrorism?
'In some ways, yes, in most ways, no.'

Do people talk about Muslims in a negative way now?
'Probably, yeah, and it's not right.'

Tom, 15

Have the attacks on September 11th changed how people feel about Muslims?
'Yes – they hate them because they hate all Christians.'

Is there a link between Islam and terrorism?
'No.'

Do people talk about Muslims in a negative way now?
'No.'

Save the Children

Alex, 15

Have the attacks on September 11th changed how people feel about Muslims?
'Some people yes, some people no. And the Americans as well.'

Why do you think this is?
'Because they feel that it's unsafe, because of certain individuals.'

Do people talk about Muslims in a negative way now?
'Not everyone, but some people do.'

Ed, 14

Have the attacks on September 11th changed how people feel about Muslims?
'Yeah, cause nobody likes Osama bin Laden, and he's Muslim.'

Is there a link between Islam and terrorism?
'Yeah, because most terrorists are harboured in Islam.'

Do people talk about Muslims in a negative way now?
'It depends where you go.'

Carly, 14

Have the attacks on September 11th changed how people feel about Muslims?
'I think they have, I'm not sure.'

Is there a link between Islam and terrorism?
'I think there is because everyone does associate terrorism with Muslims and Islam.'

Do people talk about Muslims in a negative way now?
'A lot. But I think they did before.'

Stephanie, 13

Have the attacks on September 11th changed how people feel about Muslims?
'I think it did because I think people blame all Muslims, for the attacks they did.'

Is there a link between Islam and terrorism?
'I guess so, because it's where it's heading back to, where the war is heading back to, to Islam.'

Do people talk about Muslims in a negative way now?
'I think they did a lot before, because of racism, but now I think it's just grown stronger and people use it as an excuse. I don't think of them in a negative way.'

Calie, 14

Have the attacks on September 11th changed how people feel about Muslims?
'Yeah, I think it did have an effect on the Muslims because now people have a different feeling towards them.'

Is there a link between Islam and terrorism?
'Yeah, I do think there is sort of a link, because that's where all the main people come from.'

Do people talk about Muslims in a negative way now?
'I think some people talk about them in a negative way, I don't, personally.'

■ Nadia, Nazia and Zarah Driver, Ghizlan Akerbousse, Adam Jogee and Alastair Robertson are members of Children's Express, a programme of learning through journalism for young people aged eight to 18. Visit www.childrens-express.org for more information.

■ The above information is from Save the Children's website which can be found at www.savethechildren.org.uk

© *Save the Children*

Islam: a home of tolerance, not fanaticism

Media speculation since the horrific terrorist attacks on America has pointed the finger at Muslims and the Arab world, and that has meant ordinary citizens of the US and other Western countries becoming easy prey for anti-faith hooligans. Shame.

Sadly, the latest horror to hit the US looks to have been caused by people of Middle Eastern origin, bearing Muslim names. Again, shame.

This fuels more hatred for a religion and a people who have nothing to do with these events. This is why I want to explain some basic facts about this noble way we call Islam, before, God forbid, another disaster occurs – next time probably aimed at Muslims.

I came to Islam in my late 20s, during my searching period as a wandering pop star. I found a religion that blended scientific reason with spiritual reality in a unifying faith far removed from the headlines of violence, destruction and terrorism.

One of the first interesting things I learned in the Koran was that the name of the faith comes from the word *salam* – peace. Far from the kind of Turko-Arab-centric message I expected, the Koran presented a belief in the universal existence of God, one God for all. It does not discriminate against peoples; it says we may be different colours and from different tribes, but we are all human and 'the best of people are the most God-conscious'.

Today, as a Muslim, I have been shattered by the horror of recent events; the display of death and indiscriminate killing we've all witnessed has dented humanity's confidence in itself. Terror on this scale affects everybody on this small planet, and no one is free from the fallout. Yet we should remember that such violence is almost an everyday occurrence in some Muslim lands: it should not be exacerbated by revenge

By Yusuf Islam
(formerly Cat Stevens)

attacks on more innocent families and communities.

Along with most Muslims, I feel it a duty to make clear that such orchestrated acts of incomprehensible carnage have nothing to do with the beliefs of most Muslims. The Koran specifically declares: 'If anyone murders an (innocent) person, it will be as if he has murdered the whole of humanity. And if anyone saves a person it will be as if he has saved the whole of humanity.'

Respect for religious values and justice is at the Koran's core

The Koran that our young people learn is full of stories and lessons from the history of humanity as a whole. The Gospels and the Torah are referred to; Jesus and Abraham are mentioned. In fact there is more mention in the Koran of the prophet Moses than of any other. It acknowledges the co-existence of other faiths, and in doing so acknowledges that other cultures can live together in peace.

'There is no compulsion in religion,' it states, meaning that people should not be compelled to change their faith. Elsewhere it states, 'To you, your religion; to me mine.'

Respect for religious values and justice is at the Koran's core. The Koranic history we teach our young provides ample examples of inter-religious and international relationships; of how to live together.

But some extremists take elements of the sacred scriptures out of context. They act as individuals, and when they can't come together as part of a political structure or consultative process, you find these dissident factions creating their own rules, contrary to the spirit of the Koran – which demands that those recognised as being in charge of Muslims must consult together regarding society's affairs. There is a whole chapter in the Koran entitled Consultation.

Communal wellbeing is central to human life, so there is a concept in Islam called *Istihsan*, which means 'to look for the common good'. Even though the Koran may lay down a diktat, scholars are also supposed to

consider the circumstances prevalent at the time. Sometimes that means choosing the lesser of two evils or even suspending legislation if necessary: for instance, a person who steals bread during a famine is not treated as a thief.

Once I wrote in a song, 'Where do the children play?' Our sympathy and thoughts go out to the families of all those who lost their lives in this tragic act of violence, as well as all those injured. But life must go on.

Children still need to play, and people need to live and learn more about their neighbours so that ignorance doesn't breed more blind fanaticism. Moderation is part of faith, so those who accuse Muslim schools of fostering fanaticism should learn a bit more about Islam.

The Prophet (peace be upon him) said, 'Ruined are those who insist on hardship in faith,' and, 'A believer remains within the scope of his religion as long as he doesn't kill another person illegally.' Such knowledge and words of guidance are desperately needed at this time, to separate fact from falsehood, and to recognise the Last Prophet's own definition of that which makes a person representative, or otherwise, of the faith he lived and the one we try to teach.

■ This article first appeared in *The Revival* and *The Guardian*.

© *Yusuf Islam*

Terrorism – what you can do at home

Simple preventative steps

■ Terrorism is a crime like any other, so follow the same precautions you normally take to avoid being the victim of a crime.

■ Continue to go about your day-to-day business in the normal way, but remain alert and vigilant. For example, keep an eye out for suspect bags, packages or vehicles, or people acting suspiciously at stations and airports, and report anything suspicious to the police or the appropriate authorities.

■ Trust your instincts; if you feel something is wrong, ring the police.

■ If you have information about possible bomb threats or other immediate threats, call 999.

■ If you have tip-offs or confidential information about possible terrorist activity, call the police anti-terrorist hotline: 0800 789 321.

Think about terrorism

■ Many terrorists seek other identities to protect themselves. Don't help them by leaving important identification documents such as passports and driving licences vulnerable to theft.

■ Terrorists need money to finance their operations. They get it by both legal and illegal means. Make sure you are not funding terrorists: take care of your credit cards and other financial records,

and do not donate or contribute to a collection if you are unsure where the money is going.

Know your environment

Most of us make familiar journeys on auto-pilot.

Take note of your surroundings on your journey to work, to the shops and the usual places you visit. Know who and what you expect to see each day within your neighbourhood and your workplace.

Security measures	
Would you like to see any of the following measures introduced or increased in shops in Great Britain?	
Any of these (Net)	88%
Extra CCTV cameras	80%
Extra security guards	66%
Routine bag searches	50%
None of these	12%
Don't know	*

ICM Research interviewed a random sample of 510 adults aged 18+ by telephone on 23-24 April 2004. Interviews were conducted across the country and the results have been weighted to the profile of all adults.

Source: ICM

Ask yourself:
■ Is there anything out of place?
■ Is there anything there that is not usually there?
■ Is your home/workplace as you left it?

Sensible precautions

It is sensible to be prepared for any emergency in the home and to make plans for any major disruption, including severe weather and floods.

In any type of emergency, you could lose access to power, water, telephones, and roads. Therefore:

■ Have on hand such items as:
■ batteries
■ a battery-powered torch
■ a battery-powered or wind-up radio
■ some ready-to-eat food, e.g. tinned food
■ a few bottles of water
■ blankets or duvets
■ Have the phone numbers of your local police, council, utility companies and family members handy in one place.
■ Make sure you know where the main switches for electricity, water and gas are located in your home, as you may need to turn them off in an emergency.

■ The above information is from the Home Office's website which can be found at www.homeoffice.gov.uk

© *Crown copyright*

Travelling

Terrorism – what you can do

Following is some basic advice for travelling at home and abroad, and a list of prohibited items that cannot be carried in your hand luggage if you are departing from UK airports.

Abroad

While the majority of visits abroad are trouble-free, it is always sensible to check the Travel section of the Foreign & Commonwealth Office website before planning a trip overseas.

It offers the following helpful information to British travellers:

- Country advice – official travel advice for more than 200 countries
- Risk of terrorism – a brief assessment of the threat worldwide
- Travel advice of foreign governments – from those that have issued advice
- Know before you go – information on how to prepare before your trip
- While you are there – general tips on laws and customs abroad
- If things go wrong – advice about what to do if something goes wrong on your trip

At home

Security levels have remained at a heightened level since the September 11 attacks, and passengers may still be experiencing delays on commercial flights to and from UK airports.

If you are intending to fly from the UK to any destination, including within the country, or if you are planning to collect incoming passengers, it is wise to check with the appropriate airlines and airports before you go.

Prohibited items

The following items cannot be carried on your person or in your hand luggage:

- toy guns (plastic or metal)
- metal knives of any length, including letter openers, nor knives of any other material, (such as polycarbonate or ceramic) that are strong enough to be used as potential weapons
- metal cutlery
- catapults

Check with your individual airline for a definitive list of what you can and cannot carry on your person, in your hand luggage, and in your checked baggage

---

- razor blades (unless permanently set into a fixed cartridge, such as a disposable razor)
- tradesmen's tools that have the potential to be used as weapons
- darts
- scissors, including manicure scissors (except where both blades are round-ended)
- hypodermic syringes (unless required for medical reasons, such as diabetes)
- knitting needles
- corkscrews
- large sporting bats and clubs (such as baseball, softball and cricket bats, and golf clubs; tennis, badminton and squash rackets are okay)
- billiard, snooker or pool cues

In general, airport managers and aircraft operators have the discretion to refuse any potential weapon.

Check with your individual airline for a definitive list of what you can and cannot carry on your person, in your hand luggage, and in your checked baggage.

More information – including links to airports and airlines – can be found on the Aviation section of the Department for Transport website.

- The above information is from the Home Office's website: www.homeoffice.gov.uk

■ While it is impossible to definitively ascertain when it was first used, that which we today call terrorism traces its roots back at least some 2,000 years. (p. 5)

■ Today, terrorism influences events on the international stage to a degree hitherto unachieved. Largely, this is due to the attacks of September 2001. (p. 8)

■ Fear is the greatest weakness of the 'free' Western world, in a media-dominated age where people no longer trust government experts nor scientists. Scare stories of terrorism travel fast and inflame the mind. (p. 13)

■ There is no identifiable enemy other than al-Qaida, an all-embracing term that is abused to wilfully and deceitfully present terrorism as a specifically Muslim problem associated with the misinterpretation of Islam. (p. 14)

■ One perception about suicide attacks is that they are carried out by individual deranged fanatics but this is almost never the case. Research on suicide attacks indicates that most terrorist operatives are psychologically normal, in the sense that psychological pathology does not seem to be present, and the attacks are virtually always premeditated. (p. 15)

■ So-called 'martyrdom' is not just a religious concept, however. The tradition of heroic martyrdom, where the hero sacrifices to save the life of his community, nation, or people, is a powerful element in many secular traditions. (p. 16)

■ According to the framework, a 'terrorist act' is one that 'may seriously damage a country or an international organisation' when the objective is: '(1) seriously intimidating a population, or (2) unduly compelling a Government or international organisation to perform or abstain from performing any act, or (3) seriously destabilising or destroying the fundamental political, constitutional, economic or social structures of a country or international organisation.' (p. 19)

■ It does not take much money to fund a terrorist attack, and terrorists are always looking for new ways to obtain and transfer funds. The effort to disrupt the flow of money to terrorists, both at home and internationally, is an important element of counter-terrorism. (p. 22)

■ The UK has fully implemented key anti-terrorist resolutions from the United Nations Security Council, which require all states to freeze terrorist finances. (p . 22)

■ Whether it is terrorist incidents, arrests, warnings from politicians or coverage of the actions carried out in the name of the 'war on terror', we have seen more sustained coverage of the issue than at any other time in the modern era. (p. 23)

■ Since January 2002, the *Times*, *Financial Times*, the *Guardian*, the *Mail* and the *Mirror*, have, between them, run an average of 400 stories about international terrorism every year. (p, 23)

■ We should also remember that, in the fight against terrorism, ideas matter. We must articulate a powerful and compelling global vision that can defeat the vivid, if extreme, visions of some terrorist groups. (p. 25)

■ To fight terrorism, we must not only fight terrorists. We have to win hearts and minds. To do this, we should act to resolve political disputes, articulate and work towards a vision of peace and development, and promote human rights. (p. 25)

■ If an individual Muslim were to commit an act of terrorism, this person would be guilty of violating the laws of Islam. (p. 26)

■ At the Muslim Council of Britain, we see it as the duty of all Britons, Muslims and non-Muslims, to work together to thwart any danger to this country and its inhabitants. (p. 28)

■ Since September 11 2001, the Government has substantially increased the country's counter-terrorism efforts and has improved contingency planning and resilience to a range of emergencies. (p. 33)

■ MI5 has published security advice for businesses and other organisations worried that they could be terrorist targets. It described the threat as 'real and serious' on a new website. A list of 10 safety tips include carrying out risk assessments, examining mail-handling procedures, checking that staff are who they say they are and protecting workers against flying glass by applying transparent anti-shatter film to windows. (p. 34)

■ Under the Anti-Terrorism, Crime and Security Act of 2001, passed in the wake of the 9/11 atrocities, foreign nationals can be held in high security British prisons merely on the basis of the suspicion of a politician. (p. 35)

■ Terrorism is a crime like any other, so follow the same precautions you normally take to avoid being the victim of a crime. (p. 38)

■ It is sensible to be prepared for any emergency in the home and to make plans for any major disruption, including severe weather and floods. (p. 38)

ADDITIONAL RESOURCES

You might like to contact the following organisations for further information. Due to the increasing cost of postage, many organisations cannot respond to enquiries unless they receive a stamped, addressed envelope.

Anti-Defamation League
Marketing & Communications
823 United Nations Plaza
New York, NY 10017
USA
E-mail: webmaster@adl.org
Website: www.adl.org
For 90 years, ADL has been combating anti-Semitism and bigotry of all kinds.

The Center for Defense Information
1779 Massachusetts Avenue, N.W.
Washington, DC 20036-2109
USA
Tel: + 1 202 332 0660
Fax: + 1 202 462 4559
E-mail: info@cdi.org
Website: www.cdi.org
The Center for Defense Information is dedicated to strengthening security through: international cooperation; reduced reliance on unilateral military power to resolve conflict; reduced reliance on nuclear weapons; a transformed and reformed military establishment; and, prudent oversight of, and spending on, defence programmes.

Congressional Research Service
101 Independence Avenue, SE
Washington, DC 20540-7500
USA
Website: www.loc.gov/crsinfo
The Congressional Research Service is where Members of Congress turn for the nonpartisan research, analysis, and information they need to make informed decisions on behalf of the American people.

Council on Foreign Relations
The Harold Pratt House
58 East 68th Street
New York, NY 10021
Tel: + 1 212 434 9400
Fax: + 1 212 434 9800
E-mail: communications@cfr.org
Website: www.cfr.org

Founded in 1921, the Council on Foreign Relations is an independent, national membership organisation and a nonpartisan centre for scholars dedicated to producing and disseminating ideas so that individual and corporate members, as well as policymakers, journalists, students, and interested citizens in the United States and other countries, can better understand the world and the foreign policy choices facing the United States and other governments.

Foreign Policy
Carnegie Endowment for International Peace
1779 Massachusetts Avenue, NW
Washington, DC 20036
USA
Tel: + 1 202 939 2230
Fax: + 1 202 483 4430
E-mail: info@ceip.org
Website: www.foreignpolicy.com/
Foreign Policy is published by the Carnegie Endowment for International Peace.

Global Change Ltd
1 Carlton Gardens
Ealing
London, W5 2AN
Website: www.globalchange.com/main.htm
Over 30,000 pages and 50 videos by Dr Dixon on future trends.

Home Office
Direct Communications Unit
7th Floor, 50 Queen Anne's Gate
London, SW1H 9AT
Tel: 0870 000 1585
Textphone: 020 7273 3476
Fax: 020 7273 2065
Email:
public.enquiries@homeoffice.gsi.gov.uk
Website: www.homeoffice.gov.uk

Works to reduce crime and the fear of crime, tackle youth crime and violent, sexual and drug-related crime, anti-social behaviour and disorder, increasing safety in the home and public spaces.

Institute of Race Relations
2-6 Leeke Street
London, WC1X 9HS
Tel: 020 7837 0041
Fax: 020 7278 0623
E-mail: info@irr.org.uk
Website: www.irr.org.uk
The Institute of Race Relations was established as an independent educational charity in 1958 to carry out research, publish and collect resources on race relations throughout the world.

Islam Guide
PO Box 343
Riyadh 11323
Saudi Arabia
E-mail: support@islam-guide.com
Website: www.islam-guide.com

The Muslim Council of Britian
Boardman House
64 Broadway, Stratford
London, E15 1NT
Tel: 020 8432 0585
Fax: 020 8432 0587
E-mail: admin@mcb.org.uk
Website: www.mcb.org.uk
Promotes cooperation, consensus and unity on Muslim affairs in the UK.

The Muslim News
PO News 380
Harrow, HA2 6LL
Tel: 020 8863 8586
Fax: 020 8863 9370
E-mail: info@muslimnews.co.uk
Website: www.muslimnews.co.uk
The Muslim News provides objective news and views of Muslims in the United Kingdom. It is the only independent monthly Muslim newspaper in the UK – it is neither backed by any country nor by any organisation or party.

INDEX

abductions by terrorists 9
Afghanistan 13, 17-18
Ahmad, Eqbal 10
air travel
    and terrorism
        basic advice 39
        fear of 3, 4, 13
        prohibited items 39
        security measures 32
aircraft, terrorist attacks using 9, 11
al-Qaeda 2, 8, 9, 11, 12, 14, 17-18
    in Afghanistan 17-18
    and bin Laden 18
    and counter-terrorism in the UK 30, 34
    and the European Union 19
    media coverage of 23
    and suicide attacks 16
    training camps 18
al-Zarqawi, Abu Musab 18
American Civil War 7
Anarchist terrorist groups 7
animals
    Muslim views of 26
    and terrorist attacks 32
Annan, Kofi 24-5
Anti-Defamation League 19-21
Assassins (eleventh-century Islamic terrorists) 1, 6, 7

Basque separatists 2, 19
Bin Laden, Osama 2, 9, 13, 17, 18, 34
bombing attacks 9, 11

Center for Defense Information 5-8, 10-12
Chechen conflict 14, 16
chemical/biological weapons, terrorist attacks using 9, 31
CIA (Central Intelligence Agency), Counterterrorist Center 1
citizenship, and the French Revolution 7
Congressional Research Service 15-16
consumer terrorism 11
Council on Foreign Relations 1, 2-3
counter-terrorism 13
    aviation security 32, 34
    contingency planning and resilience 33
    counter-terrorist measures in London 31-2
    and the European Union 19-21
    and Islam 26, 28-9
    MI5 safety tips 34
    public attitudes to 35
    security measures 38
    targeting terrorist funds 22
    UK legislation 30, 33-4
        Anti-Terrorism, Crime and Security Act (2001) 27-8, 30, 34, 35
        Civil Contingencies Bill 34
        and internment 30, 35

numbers arrested under 29
        Proceeds of Crime Act 22
        Terrorism Act (2000) 28, 30, 33-4
    and the United Nations 24-5
    White convictions in the UK 27-8
crime, terrorism and organised crime 22

economic inequality, and terrorism 13, 21
economic terrorism 11
European Arrest Warrant 19, 20
European Convention on Human Rights, and UK
    terrorism laws 30, 35
European Union
    response to terrorism 19-21
        list of designated foreign terrorist organisations 19-20

fear of terrorism 3-5, 13
French Revolution, and terror 1, 6-7, 10, 14

Germany, Nazi 7

human rights, and terrorism 25

IMRO (Macedonian Revolutionary Organization) 7
India
    terrorism in 7
        Thuggee cult 1, 6
Indonesia, terrorism in 14
Institute of Race Relations 27-8
IRA (Irish Republican Army) 2, 11, 23
Iran, state-sponsored terrorism in 3
Iraq, and terrorism 13, 14, 16
Islam
    and terrorism 13
        condemnation of 26, 28-9, 37-8
        convictions of Muslims in the UK 27
Islamic terrorist groups
    Assassins 1, 6, 7, 16
    Hamas 2, 16
    objectives of 18
    suicide attacks by 16
    Tauhid 18
    see also al-Qaeda
Islamophobia 36
Israeli terrorist groups 2-3, 14
Italy, Fascist 7

Japan
    atomic bombs dropped in 8
    terrorism in 7
        Arum Shinrikyo cult 3
Jewish terrorist groups 2-3
    in first-century Palestine 1, 6

kidnappings by terrorists 9
Koran see Quran (Koran)

Ku Klux Klan 7
Kurdistan Workers' Party 2

League of Nations 7
Liberty 35
Libya 11, 24
London, counter-terrorism measures in 31-2

martyrdom, and suicide attacks 16
Marxism, and terrorism 7
media
    coverage of terrorism 10, 23-4, 27, 28-9, 37
        and smallpox vaccinations 31
Muhammad, Prophet 26, 28, 38
Muslim Council of Britain 28-9
Muslim News 14

nacro-terrorism 11
nationalist terrorism 2, 7
NHS (National Health Service), and counter-terrorism 33
Northern Ireland 2, 7, 8, 11, 14
    convictions of Loyalists under the Terrorism Act
        (2000) 27, 28

Ottoman Empire, and terrorism 7

Palestinian terrorist groups
    first-century 1
    Hamas 2, 20, 21
    and suicide attacks 15-16
PLO (Palestine Liberation Organisation) 1, 2, 16
police
    and counter-terrorism 33, 34, 38
        and the European Union 20, 21
        and the Muslim community 28, 29

Quran (Koran), and terrorism 26, 29, 37

religious terrorism 2-3, 6
    and suicide attacks 15-16
Russia
    Chechen conflict 14, 16
    massacre in Beslan 14
    Narodnaya Volya ('People's Will') 1, 7
    Stalinist 7

Saddam Hussein 18
Saudi Arabia, terrorist attacks in 9
schools, emergency plans in the event of a terrorist attack
    32
Second World War, and terrorism 7, 8
September 11 2001 terrorist attacks 8, 9, 11, 13, 14, 16,
    22
    and counter-terrorism
        in the European Union 19, 21
        in the UK 30, 31-2, 33-4, 35
    and Islamophobia 36
Serbia, terrorist groups in 1, 7
shootings
    by terrorists 9
    'sniper' murders in Washington DC 11

Sicari (early Jewish terrorists) 1, 6, 7
smallpox vaccinations 31
South America, military dictatorships 7
Spain
    Basque separatists 2, 19
    Madrid rail bombings (2004) 19, 21, 23, 28, 29
sporting events, avoiding due to fear of terrorism 3, 4
state-sponsored terrorism 3, 7-8, 11
suicide terrorists 9, 15-16, 21
    profile of 16

Tamil Tigers 16
terrorism
    audiences for 1
    brief history of 5-8
    deaths caused by 34
    defining 1, 10-12, 19
    different types of 2
    European Union response to 19-21
    fear of 3-5, 13
    four key elements of 1
    frequently asked questions about 31-2
    and guerrilla warfare 12
    media coverage of 10, 23-4, 27, 28-9
    methods of attack 9, 11-12
    origins of the word 1
    and political violence 10-11, 12
    preparing for emergencies in the home 38
    strategy behind 1
    see also al-Qaeda; counter-terrorism; September 11
        2001 terrorist attacks
Thuggee cult in India 1, 6
totalitarian regimes, and terrorism 7
travel
    and terrorism
        basic advice 39
        fear of 3, 4, 13
tribalism, and terrorism 13
Turkey, terrorist attack on HSBC Bank in Istanbul 9

United Nations, and counter-terrorism 22, 24-5
United States
    and terrorism
        and the American Civil War 7
        anti-terrorism laws 11
        and the European Union 21
        fear of 3-5, 13
        Global War on 8
        Guantanamo Bay detention facility 11, 35
        and the Lockerbie bombing 11
        media coverage of 23
        'sniper' murders in Washington DC 11

war, and terrorism 10, 11, 13
widows, suicide attacks by 15
women, suicide attacks by 15

young people, attitudes to Islam and terrorism 36

Zealots (early Jewish terrorists) 1, 6, 7
Zimbabwe 7

ACKNOWLEDGEMENTS

The publisher is grateful for permission to reproduce the following material.

While every care has been taken to trace and acknowledge copyright, the publisher tenders its apology for any accidental infringement or where copyright has proved untraceable. The publisher would be pleased to come to a suitable arrangement in any such case with the rightful owner.

Chapter One: An Overview

Terrorism, © 2004 Council on Foreign Relations, Reprinted with permission, *Types of terrorism*, © 2004 Council on Foreign Relations, Reprinted with permission, *Fear of terrorism*, © 2004 Harris Interactive Inc. All rights reserved. Reproduction prohibited without the express permission of Harris Interactive. EOE M/F/D/V, *A brief history of terrorism*, © The Center for Defense Information, *Methods of attack*, © Crown copyright is reproduced with the permission of Her Majesty's Stationery Office, *Terrorism: the problems of definition*, © The Center for Defense Information, *The war against terrorism*, © Dr Patrick Dixon, *The unrealistic war on terror*, © The Muslim News, *Terrorists and suicide attacks*, © Congressional Research Service, *Think again: Al Qaeda*, © 2004 foreignpolicy.com, *The European Union response to terrorism*, © Anti-Defamation League, *Terrorism and the EU*, © ICM Research, *Targeting terrorist funds*, © Crown copyright is reproduced with the permission of Her Majesty's Stationery Office, *At the service of politicians*, © Guardian Newspapers Limited 2004, *Threat of terrorism* © ICM Research, *Ability to reason vital in fighting terrorism*, © United Nations, *What does Islam say about terrorism?*, © www.islam-guide.com

Chapter Two: Terrorism and the UK

Who are the terrorists?, © Institute of Race Relations, *'We must unite to defeat this threat'*, © The Muslim Council of Britain, *Home Office draw up tighter terrorism laws*, © Guardian Newspapers Limited 2004, *Terrorism*, © Crown copyright is reproduced with the permission of Her Majesty's Stationery Office, *Counter-terrorism and resilience: key facts*, © Crown copyright is reproduced with the permission of Her Majesty's Stationery Office, *MI5 website lists 10 anti-terrorist tips*, © Telegraph Group Limited, London 2004, *Internment in Britain*, © Liberty, *Countering terrorism*, © ICM Research, *Islamophobia – what is it?*, © Save the Children, *Islam: a home of tolerance, not fanaticism*, © Yusuf Islam, *Terrorism – what you can do at home*, © Crown copyright is reproduced with the permission of Her Majesty's Stationery Office, *Travelling*, © Crown copyright is reproduced with the permission of Her Majesty's Stationery Office.

Photographs and illustrations:

Pages 1, 10, 18, 25, 37, 39: Simon Kneebone; pages 2, 14, 22, 26: Angelo Madrid; pages 5, 31: Pumpkin House; pages 6, 12, 20, 27: Don Hatcher; pages 9, 16, 29: Bev Aisbett.

Craig Donnellan
Cambridge
January, 2005